This

Sandra Lee
semi-homemade®

cooking made light

book belongs to:

....

Meredith® Books Des Moines, Iowa
Copyright © 2006 Sandra Lee Semi-Homemade® All rights reserved. Printed in the U.S.A.
Library of Congress Control Number 2006930036 ISBN-13: 978-0-696-23266-4 ISBN-10: 0-696-23266-9

25 Tropical Fruit Parfait

61 Cajun Salmon Salad

88 BBQ Turkey Pizza

173 Adobo Beef

214 Super Moist Chocolate Cake

sem·i·home·made

adj. **1:** a stress-free solution-based formula that provides savvy shortcuts and affordable, timesaving tips for overextended do-it-yourself homemakers **2:** a quick and easy equation wherein 70% ready-made convenience products are added to 30% fresh ingredients with creative personal style, allowing homemakers to take 100% of the credit for something that looks, feels, or tastes homemade **3:** a foolproof resource for having it all—and having the time to enjoy it **4:** a method created by Sandra Lee for home, garden, crafts, beauty, food, fashion, and entertaining wherein everything looks, tastes, and feels as if it was made from scratch.

Solution-based **E**nterprise that **M**otivates, **I**nspires, and **H**elps **O**rganize and **M**anage time, while **E**nriching **M**odern life by **A**dding **D**ependable shortcuts **E**veryday.

dedication

To my sisters Kimber and Cindy and my brothers Rich and John
for teaching me everything that is truly important.
May your lives always be happy and healthy.
I love you more then the moon and the stars!
–Sandy

with great gratitude

To my Grandma Lorraine:
for trying to teach me "good food habits"

special thanks

To my deliciously helpful and healthful publishing family:
Jack, Bob, Doug, Jim, Jan, Ken, Jeff, Mick, and Jessica
Jeff: Culinary Director
Pamela, Mark, Laurent, Michael, and Lisa

Table of Contents

Chapter 1

Breakfasts &
Smoothies
16

Chapter 2

Starters &
Snacks
32

Chapter 3

Salads &
Soups
48

Chapter 4

Pastas &
Pizzas
70

Letter from Sandra

We all want to eat healthier, cook healthier, be healthier! I find this to be especially true when I'm cooking for someone else. Cooking with my nieces and nephews has made me more conscientious about the food I put into my body—and into theirs. I do a lot of work with and for children, so I get a firsthand look at the difference nutrition makes in all our lives. We teach our kids to eat what we eat, and lessons learned early on stay with us for life. Reading food labels, buying organic, pesticide-free foods, and stocking the pantry with healthful meal starters puts everyone on the path to living longer, healthier, happier lives.

The turning point for me was the Twinkie® Cake. My nephew Bryce was joining me on my Food Network show to make a Twinkie® Cake for Mother's Day. Cute idea, right? Not when I started to think about the mounds and mounds of buttery cake, filled with thousands of frosted sugary calories … yum … YUCK! What in the world was I teaching my 6-year old nephew about eating? I decided we'd make a bran muffin shortcake instead. We layered fiber-filled bran muffins with juicy, vitamin-rich strawberries and fluffs of "lite" whipped topping embellished with a touch of vanilla extract. Still scrumptious and not nearly as naughty. And it was more fun to make!

Healthy living can be simple and fun. I've learned from experience that if something takes too much time or is perceived as a chore, it won't get done. Too often, people view healthy eating as a short-term solution rather than a long-term goal. *Semi-Homemade® Light Cooking* makes it doable every day, pairing realistic recipes with readily available supermarket foods to make delicious, nutritious meals you can feel good about serving. It's all based on my 70/30 philosophy: Mix 30% fresh ingredients with 70% quality convenience foods to create wholesome, no-hassle dishes that fit even the most hectic lifestyle.

Whether you're feeding a family, entertaining friends, or starting the journey to a whole new you, the road to good health goes right through the kitchen. This book has 10 chapters filled with delicious, good-for-you foods, including soups and salads, sides and meats, even snacks and desserts—everything you need to eat satisfying, balanced meals and munchies all day long. Eat a wide variety of foods, focus on fruits and vegetables, and add low-fat dairy products and lean meat, poultry, and fish for essential protein. Fix the foods you like: More than 115 recipes in this book show you how to cut fat, sodium, and cholesterol from your favorite foods without sacrificing flavor or giving up taste. And every chapter helps you control portions, make savvy substitutions, and use the healthiest cooking techniques to create a beautiful, mouthwatering meal that will make you feel as good as your food looks.

I hope this book will be *your* Twinkie® Cake—the turning point to a new way of living. Food is a friend and the foundation for life, so make it a healthy relationship. Eat well. Live better. Look great. Feel fabulous … the Semi-Homemade® way.

Cheers to a happy, healthy life!

Sandra Lee

Super Foods and Flavors

Pantry Power

A smartly stocked pantry is the gateway to good health. When it's full of healthful ingredients, you can't help making smart dining decisions. The following foods are the perfect ingredients to stock up on—what I call "Super Foods." They're the supermarket superstars, boosting your energy, lowering your risk of certain diseases, and giving you more vitamins and nutrients than other foods. Choose foods you can feel good about eating every day—unsweetened juices, low-salt vegetables, and fat-free dressings. To fill up on flavor, not fat, stock a wide variety of spices and seasonings for mixers and toppers. Garbanzo beans, roasted red peppers, sun-dried tomatoes, and artichoke hearts mix with chunky sauces, whole grain couscous, rice, and pasta to contribute good carbs and protein. Exotic ingredients, like mango nectar, coconut milk, and soy sauce, take the simplest of meals from mundane to marvelous. Pair these easy-to-find foods with fresh meats and vegetables in my easy-to-fix recipes and you'll have everything you need to cook quick, eat light and healthy, and feel fabulous.

Soybeans & tofu

Tuna & salmon

Praise for Protein

Protein is essential for the body to repair tissue and build muscle. The following lean proteins are best:

Eggs also supply vitamins A, B_6, B_{12}, and folate; iron; phosphorous; and zinc. Eat as many egg whites as you like but stick to four whole eggs or less per week.

Tuna and salmon contain omega-3 fatty acids, which lower cholesterol levels and reduce risk of heart disease.

Soybeans and tofu are great at lowering "bad" LDL cholesterol levels in the bloodstream. They also may help reduce the risk of certain cancers.

Skinless, boneless poultry is relatively lean but should be eaten in moderation.

Eggs

Super Fruits

Sweet, juicy, and oh so delicious—fresh fruit is a dessert in itself.

Apricots are high in beta-carotene, fiber, and vitamin C.

Bananas are packed with magnesium and potassium.

Berries are antioxidant powerhouses.

Citrus fruits have plenty of vitamin C.

Cranberries are full of phenols, which lower oxidation of LDL cholesterol.

Mangoes contain bioflavonoids that aid the immune system.

Pineapples contain enzymes that help combat allergies and other ailments.

Tomatoes are technically a fruit and are packed with the antioxidant lycopene.

Tomatoes

Pineapple

Berries

Cranberries

Mangoes, kiwis & papayas

Citrus fruits

Apricots

Bananas

Broccoli

Super Vegetables

When Mom said "eat your veggies," she knew what she was talking about! Vegetables are the best super foods available. Fresh is best, but canned and frozen work well too.

Broccoli is packed with fiber and vitamins A and C.

Carrots are filled with beta-carotene, which can reduce the risk of stroke.

Chile peppers not only add irresistible heat and flavor to recipes but also contain the antioxidant capsaicin.

Garlic is a must for the rich, vibrant flavors found in many savory dishes, but it may also lower cholesterol and blood pressure. It also contains chemicals that may destroy cancer cells.

Onions are extremely versatile and can be added to a plethora of dishes. They also contain sulphur compounds and the flavonoid quercetin, which may have anticancer properties.

Mushrooms have beta-glucan, which stimulates the immune system.

Spinach is filled with vitamins A and C, folic acid, and magnesium, which may help control cancer.

Sweet potatoes are considered one of the most healthful vegetables available and contain 360% of the daily value of vitamin A.

Chile peppers

Spinach

Mushrooms

Garlic

Sweet potatoes

Onions

Grains Are Good

Carbs got a bad rap a few years ago, but they're back with a vengeance. It's the refined carbs (white pasta, rice, and bread) that lack fiber and nutrients, so always choose whole grain options.

Multigrain bread: If you missed bread during the no-carb craze, you'll be glad to know it's good for you. Choose multigrain or whole grain and you'll be adding B vitamins, which may lower the risk of heart disease.

Legumes are high in protein and contain both soluble and insoluble fiber.

Whole grains include wheat, oats, corn, brown rice, barley, rye, and quinoa—as long as "whole" is in the name, it's good.

Legumes

Multigrain bread

Whole grains

Catch-All Category

Certain other foods don't fit in the previous categories but are still nutritious and healthful.

Green and black teas contain polyphenols (antioxidants), which may reduce heart disease and cancer.

Dark chocolate and cocoa have antioxidants and flavanols, which improve blood flow.

Ginger contains antioxidants that have been shown to fight cancer.

Cinnamon may lower blood sugar levels (eat ½ teaspoon per day).

Nuts

Dark chocolate & cocoa   **Ginger**   **Cinnamon**

The Facts on Fat

Fat is fat is fat … or is it? In truth, there are good fats and bad fats (or at least not-so-good fats).

Monounsaturated and polyunsaturated fats are both healthful. Monounsaturated fats include olive, canola, and peanut oils and help lower LDL (bad) cholesterol and raise HDL (good) cholesterol, which can help lower the risk of heart disease. Polyunsaturated fats are found in corn, safflower, sunflower, flaxseed, and soybean oils, as well as in fatty fish, such as salmon and tuna (see page 9) in the form of omega-3 fatty acids. These will help lower total cholesterol.

Plant sterols are found in nuts and seeds. They slow the absorption of cholesterol and lower LDL levels.

Saturated and trans fats are the "unfriendly" fats. Poultry skin (eat skinless!), butter, and full-fat dairy products are loaded with saturated fats. Trans fats are found in stick margarines, shortening, and many processed foods. Both fats raise bad cholesterol.

Cholesterol is found in egg yolks (egg whites are fine), liver, shellfish, and full-fat dairy products. Cholesterol-rich foods can raise cholesterol in some people, but they don't affect everyone.

Good fats

Bad fats

The Teaspoon Test

"Healthy" foods can be loaded with sugar, so read the labels, then do the teaspoon test. A teaspoon of sugar equals 4 grams or 16 calories. A 2,000-calorie-per-day diet should include no more than 8 to 10 teaspoons—or 32 to 40 grams—per day of added sugar. That's about 6 to 8% of the day's total calories. Eight ounces of frozen yogurt equals 8.5 teaspoons, and one 16-ounce bottle of sugary juice drink equals 11.5 teaspoons—way over the recommended daily allowance. Check the label carefully. Sugars are also called honey, fructose, dextrose, glucose, sucrose, maltose, molasses, corn syrup, fruit juice concentrate, maltitol, sorbitol, mannitol, xylitol, erythritol, and lactitol.

Sodium Check

Healthy adults should not eat more than 2,300 mg of sodium per day. One teaspoon of table salt contains about that amount. If you're watching your sodium, double check the sodium content on packaged goods. Whenever possible, select reduced-, low-sodium, or no-salt-added options. Even these products can be high. Moderation is key, if you eat high-sodium foods one day, lower your sodium the next.

Shop Smart

Eating right starts in the supermarket. Organic foods are the best bargain; while slightly more expensive, they offer more nutrition without harmful pesticide residue or excess additives. If you can't buy organic, select the least-processed brand. And always check out a food's nutritional profile by comparing:

The Nutrition Facts Label: Labels are standardized to make comparing brands easy. Avoid "High Fives"—high numbers for calories, sugars, sodium, fats, and cholesterol. Do the math and don't be fooled. That "diet" cookie might be fat-free, but if it's loaded with sugar and has 70 calories per serving—and there are four servings per cookie—it's not such a find.

The Ingredients List: Ingredients are listed in order of weight. Look for proteins and good carbs, such as whole grains, fruits, or vegetables, to lead the list. If refined sugars, enriched (white) flours, sodium, nitrates (preservatives), or bad fats, like saturated or trans fats, are the main ingredients, keep looking.

Ten Simple Steps to a Healthier Life

You don't have to spend hours in the kitchen—or a fortune in the supermarket—to put a nutritious meal on the table. You just have to make good choices. My 70/30 philosophy makes it easy to be fit and healthful. Eat 70% complex carbohydrates, protein, and low-fat dairy plus 30% healthy fats (with risky trans and saturated fats only 30% of that) to look and feel 100% terrific every day. Start today with these ten simple steps:

1. Swap when you shop. Replace full-fat milks, cheeses, mayonnaise, dressings, breads, and crackers with their lighter versions.

2. Buy organic. Your body—and the environment—will thank you. Organic foods might cost a little more, but the large chains have made them more affordable. Soak and wash produce in salty water to remove any of nature's little friends.

3. Cook lighter by reducing the use of fat. Steaming, poaching, broiling, grilling, and baking are all good options. Forget butter and lard— use heart-friendly olive, canola, corn, safflower, or soybean oil instead.

4. Make food multitask. Don't think of fruits and vegetables as a side dish—use them as toppings, garnishes, sauces, desserts, and snacks. A salad, chicken with vegetable sauce, and sorbet with berries gives you your 4 to 5 servings. Crudités (raw vegetables) and salsa get you halfway there.

5. Be selective about starches. Eat good carbs, such as whole grain breads, cereals, and pastas, every day. Cut back on refined white flours. Update favorite foods with spinach and sun-dried tomato pastas, whole wheat pizza crust, and a mix of whole wheat and white flour when baking.

6. Pass on the salt ... and say "yes" to good sugar. Buy reduced-sodium products and watch nutrition labels to limit your intake to 1,500 mg per day. Try to get most of your sugar from fruit, but don't cut dessert out of your diet. You may end up bingeing instead.

7. Eat foods you like. Taste is learned, so train your taste buds to like foods that are good for you. If you can't learn to like it, find something else.

8. Prepare a colorful plate. Different-color foods provide different nutrients, so eat a wide variety. When you serve dinner, make sure the largest percentage of your plate is filled with vegetables. Meat and starch—such as rice or bread—should be served in small portions. Also, make each of your 4 to 5 fruits and vegetables a different color and you'll reap the benefits.

9. Pay attention to how much and how you eat. Know how much a serving is and stick to it. Buy smaller plates and chew slowly, savoring every bite. You'll fill up faster and digest food better.

10. Be a semi-vegetarian. Eat vegetarian-only meals one or two days a week or have meat-based meals only once or twice a week. Eat mostly fish and skinless poultry.

Most important, try not to focus on food; instead focus on enjoying life to the fullest. Be active about what you eat and do and remember to exercise regularly. You'll look, feel, and be better for it!

Breakfasts & Smoothies

There's a reason they call it a Power Breakfast. I know I wouldn't have the energy to power through a hectic day without one! To make breakfast a priority, make it part of your morning routine. Get dressed, make the bed, whip up a Tropical Fruit Parfait. Think outside the cereal box with make-ahead muffins with zucchini and bran or carrots and coconut—both are bursting with filling fiber that will head off a midmorning snack. When you can barely find five minutes to spare, make a Peach-Mango Smoothie or a Kiwi Kooler to turbocharge breakfast in one gulp-and-go glass. Protein-packed eggs can curb your appetite all day, so take advantage of the weekend and linger over a Smoked Salmon Omelet or a Florentine Scramble. Monday through Sunday, breakfast sets the pace, so start smart and you'll reap the benefits.

The Recipes

Smoked Salmon Omelet

Start to Finish 15 minutes
Makes 2 servings

3	tablespoons light sour cream, *Horizon Organic*®
½	teaspoon Dijon mustard, *Grey Poupon*®
½	teaspoon dried dillweed, *McCormick*®
	Olive oil cooking spray, *Mazola® Pure*
⅔	cup 100-percent liquid egg whites, *All Whites*®
¼	cup light cream cheese with chives and onion, softened, *Kraft*®
2	ounces thinly sliced smoked salmon (lox-style)
1	tablespoon black lumpfish caviar, *Romanoff*® (optional)
	Fresh chives (optional)

1. In a small bowl, stir together sour cream, mustard, and dillweed; set aside.

2. Coat an 8-inch nonstick skillet with cooking spray; heat over medium heat. Add ⅓ cup of the egg whites; cover. Cook for 2 to 4 minutes or until egg whites have set. Spoon half of the cream cheese and half of the sliced salmon onto the half of the omelet farthest from the handle. Tilt the pan over serving plate and scoot the omelet out of pan, folding it in half as it slides out of pan. Repeat with remaining egg whites, cream cheese, and salmon.

3. Top omelets with sour cream mixture. Serve with caviar and fresh chives (optional).

NOTE: This makes a great brunch dish when served with a tossed salad.

Per serving 160 cal., 8 g total fat (4 g sat. fat), 28 mg chol., 916 mg sodium, 5 g carbo., 0 g fiber, 17 g pro.
Daily Values 7% vit. A, 1% vit. C, 13% calcium, 2% iron

Florentine Scramble

Start to Finish 15 minutes
Makes 4 servings

1 ½   cups refrigerated egg product, *Egg Beaters*®
¼   cup finely chopped fresh basil
1   tablespoon grated Parmesan cheese, *DiGiorno*®
⅓   cup frozen cut spinach, cooked, *Birds Eye*®
½   cup petite diced tomatoes with sweet onion and garlic, drained, *S&W*®
  Butter-flavor cooking spray, *Mazola® Pure*

SUPER FOODS
Eggs
Spinach
Tomatoes

1. In a small bowl, stir together egg product, basil, and Parmesan cheese; set aside.

2. Squeeze any excess water from spinach; place in a microwave-safe bowl. Stir in tomatoes. Cover and microwave on high setting (100% power) for 1 minute; set aside.

3. Coat a medium nonstick skillet with cooking spray; heat over medium heat. Pour egg mixture into pan. As egg starts to set, scramble using a wooden spoon or spatula.

4. When eggs are almost cooked, sprinkle in spinach and tomatoes. Fold until combined and eggs are just cooked through. Do not overcook eggs or they will become watery.

Per serving 67 cal., 0 g total fat (0 g sat. fat), 1 mg chol., 344 mg sodium, 5 g carbo., 1 g fiber, 10 g pro.
Daily Values 67% vit. A, 5% vit. C, 8% calcium, 12% iron

Carrot-Coconut Muffins

Prep 10 minutes **Bake** 18 minutes
Cool 5 minutes **Makes** 12 muffins

SUPER FOODS
Carrots
Apple
Cinnamon
Ginger

Canola oil cooking spray, *Mazola® Pure*
1 box (19-ounce) fat-free apple cinnamon muffin mix, *Krusteaz®*
4 jars (4 ounces each) organic carrot baby food (pureed), *Earth's Best®*
1 cup shredded coconut, *Baker's®*
¼ cup apple juice, *Tree Top®*
1 teaspoon ground cinnamon, *McCormick®*
½ teaspoon ground ginger, *McCormick®*

1. Preheat oven to 400 degrees F. Lightly coat twelve 2½-inch muffin cups with cooking spray; set aside.

2. In a large bowl, stir together muffin mix, carrot baby food, coconut, apple juice, cinnamon, and ginger until combined. Spoon batter into prepared muffin cups, filling each two-thirds full.

3. Bake muffins in preheated oven for 18 to 20 minutes or until tops are golden brown. Cool muffins in muffin cups on a wire rack for 5 minutes. Remove from muffin cups. Serve warm.

Per muffin 177 cal., 2 g total fat (2 g sat. fat), 0 mg chol., 295 mg sodium, 36 g carbo., 3 g fiber, 3 g pro.
Daily Values 87% vit. A, 4% vit. C, 3% calcium, 6% iron

Moist Zucchini-Bran Muffins

Prep 15 minutes **Bake** 20 minutes
Cool 5 minutes **Makes** 12 muffins

SUPER FOODS
Whole grains
Apple
Eggs
Cinnamon

Canola oil cooking spray, *Mazola® Pure*
1 box (18.25-ounce) raisin bran muffin mix, *Sun-Maid®*
1¼ cups grated zucchini (about 1 medium zucchini)
¾ cup apple juice, *Tree Top®*
2 egg whites
¼ cup unsweetened applesauce, *Tree Top®*
1 teaspoon ground cinnamon, *McCormick®*
Honey (optional)

1. Preheat oven to 400 degrees F. Lightly coat twelve 2½-inch muffin cups with cooking spray; set aside.

2. In a large bowl, stir together muffin mix, zucchini, apple juice, egg whites, applesauce, and cinnamon until combined. Spoon batter into prepared muffin cups, filling each two-thirds full.

3. Bake muffins in preheated oven for 20 to 22 minutes or until tops are golden brown. Cool muffins in muffin cups on a wire rack for 5 minutes. Remove from muffin cups. Serve warm. Drizzle with honey (optional).

Per muffin 184 cal., 2 g total fat (1 g sat. fat), 0 mg chol., 246 mg sodium, 39 g carbo., 3 g fiber, 3 g pro.
Daily Values 1% vit. A, 5% vit. C, 8% calcium, 1% iron

Tropical Fruit Parfait

Start to Finish 10 minutes
Makes 2 servings

1   cup fat-free vanilla yogurt, *Dannon®*
2   teaspoons lime juice, *ReaLime®*
     Pinch cayenne pepper, *McCormick®*
1   can (15.25-ounce) tropical fruit salad, drained, *Dole®*
1   cup low-fat granola cereal, *Quaker®*
     Fresh raspberries (optional)
     Fresh mint sprigs (optional)

SUPER FOODS
Yogurt
Citrus
Pineapple
Mango
Oats

1. In a small bowl, stir together yogurt, lime juice, and cayenne pepper; set aside.

2. Divide half of the fruit salad between 2 parfait or wine glasses. Spoon ¼ cup of the yogurt mixture over fruit in each. Top each with ¼ cup granola. Repeat layers.

3. Top parfaits with raspberries and mint (optional).

Per serving 361 cal., 3 g total fat (1 g sat. fat), 2 mg chol., 215 mg sodium, 79 g carbo., 5 g fiber, 8 g pro.
Daily Values 20% vit. A, 93% vit. C, 20% calcium, 17% iron

Pumpkin Pie Oatmeal

Start to Finish 5 minutes
Makes 2 servings

Pumpkins are a scrumptious source of beta-carotene, and cholesterol-squelching oatmeal contributes fiber. Made with quick oats, fat-free milk, and pecans, it's a hot, hearty breakfast in only 5 minutes.

SUPER FOODS
Pumpkin
Oats
Pecans

1   can (12-ounce) fat-free evaporated milk, *Carnation®*
½   cup pumpkin pie filling, *Libby's®*
1¼ cups quick-cooking oats, *Quaker®*
3   tablespoons chopped pecans, *Planters®*

1. In a saucepan, combine evaporated milk and pumpkin pie filling. Bring to a boil over medium-high heat. Add oats; cook and stir for 1 minute or until thickened. Stir in 2 tablespoons of the pecans. Top each serving with some of the remaining 1 tablespoon pecans.

Per serving 458 cal., 11 g total fat (1 g sat. fat), 7 mg chol., 283 mg sodium, 70 g carbo., 7 g fiber, 20 g pro.
Daily Values 127% vit. A, 4% vit. C, 50% calcium, 19% iron

Pineapple-Coconut Smoothie

Start to Finish 10 minutes
Makes 2 servings

SUPER FOODS
Pineapple
Yogurt

$3/4$ **cup fat-free milk**
$1/2$ **cup light coconut milk, *A Taste of Thai*®**
$1/3$ **cup unsweetened pineapple juice, *Dole*®**
$1 1/2$ **cups ice**
1   **can (8-ounce) crushed pineapple (juice pack), drained, *Dole*®**
1   **small banana, chopped**
1   **container (6-ounce) fat-free vanilla yogurt, *Dannon*®**
1   **tablespoon packed brown sugar, *C&H*®**
  Fresh pineapple wedges (optional)

1. Pour milk, coconut milk, and pineapple juice into a blender. Add ice, pineapple, banana, yogurt, and brown sugar. Cover and blend on high for 1 minute or until smooth.

2. Pour into glasses. Serve with pineapple wedges (optional).

Per serving 275 cal., 3 g total fat (2 g sat. fat), 2 mg chol., 103 mg sodium, 55 g carbo., 3 g fiber, 8 g pro.
Daily Values 5% vit. A, 33% vit. C, 25% calcium, 7% iron

Peach-Mango Smoothie

Start to Finish 5 minutes
Makes 1 serving

SUPER FOODS
Mango
Yogurt
Soy

$1/2$ **cup mango nectar, *Kern's*®**
1   **cup ice**
1   **container (6-ounce) fat-free peach yogurt, *Dannon*®**
$1/2$ **cup frozen mango chunks, *Dole*®**
$1/2$ **cup frozen peach slices, *Dole*®**
$1/4$ **block soft silken tofu, chopped, *Mori-Nu*®**
  Frozen mango chunks, *Dole*® (optional)
  Frozen peach slices, *Dole*® (optional)
  Maraschino cherries (optional)

1. Pour mango nectar into a blender. Add ice, yogurt, the $1/2$ cup mango chunks, $1/2$ cup peach slices, and tofu. Cover and blend on high for 30 seconds to 1 minute or until smooth.

2. Pour into a glass. Serve with additional mango chunks, additional peach slices, and maraschino cherries (optional).

Per serving 300 cal., 3 g total fat (0 g sat. fat), 3 mg chol., 111 mg sodium, 61 g carbo., 3 g fiber, 11 g pro.
Daily Values 37% vit. A, 82% vit. C, 24% calcium, 4% iron

Banana-Date Blast

Start to Finish 15 minutes
Makes 2 servings

²/₃	cup water
1	packet (1.19-ounce) low-sugar maple and brown sugar instant oatmeal, *Quaker*®
1	small banana
1	cup ice
³/₄	cup unsweetened vanilla soymilk, *WestSoy*®
¹/₃	cup finely chopped dates, *Sunsweet*®
	Banana, chopped (optional)
	Dates, finely chopped (optional)

SUPER FOODS
Oats
Banana
Soy

1. In a microwave bowl, combine water and oatmeal packet. Cover and microwave on high setting (100% power) for 1 to 2 minutes; cool to room temperature.

2. In a blender, combine cooled oatmeal, the 1 small banana, ice, soymilk, and the ¹/₃ cup dates. Cover and blend until smooth and frothy. Pour into 2 glasses. Serve with additional banana and dates (optional).

Per serving 252 cal., 2 g total fat (0 g sat. fat), 0 mg chol., 170 mg sodium, 57 g carbo., 5 g fiber, 6 g pro.
Daily Values 11% vit. A, 9% vit. C, 10% calcium, 15% iron

Polar Mocha

Start to Finish 5 minutes
Makes 1 serving

Some like it hot; others prefer cold. This undeniably cool coffee confection perks up your morning with a brew that's fashionably frothy. Nonfat yogurt and soymilk give it coffeehouse taste—and calcium too.

1¹/₂	cups ice
1	cup fat-free vanilla yogurt, *Dannon*®
¹/₂	cup unsweetened vanilla soymilk, *WestSoy*®
2	tablespoons chocolate-flavored syrup, *Hershey's*®
1	teaspoon instant coffee crystals, *Folgers*®
	Chocolate-covered espresso beans (optional)

SUPER FOODS
Yogurt
Soy

1. Place ice in a blender. Add yogurt, soymilk, chocolate-flavored syrup, and coffee crystals. Cover and blend on high for 1 minute or until smooth. Pour into a glass. Top with espresso beans (optional).

Per serving 287 cal., 3 g total fat (0 g sat. fat), 4 mg chol., 180 mg sodium, 50 g carbo., 3 g fiber, 14 g pro.
Daily Values 9% vit. A, 24% calcium, 10% iron

Rootin'-Tootin' Raspberry Burst

Start to Finish 5 minutes
Makes 1 serving

SUPER FOODS
Strawberry
Yogurt
Raspberries
Banana

½ cup strawberry nectar, *Kern's*®
1 container (6-ounce) fat-free raspberry yogurt, *Dannon*®
¾ cup frozen raspberries, *Dole*®
¾ cup ice
½ of a small banana
Fresh raspberries and/or strawberries (optional)

1. Pour strawberry nectar into a blender. Add yogurt, frozen raspberries, ice, and banana. Cover and blend on high for 1 minute or until smooth.

2. Pour into a glass. Serve with fresh berries (optional).

Per serving 268 cal., 0 g total fat (0 g sat. fat), 3 mg chol., 145 mg sodium, 60 g carbo., 5 g fiber, 8 g pro.
Daily Values 8% vit. A, 62% vit. C, 18% calcium, 6% iron

Kiwi Kooler

Start to Finish 10 minutes
Makes 2 servings

SUPER FOODS
Kiwifruits
Yogurt
Citrus

1 cup guava nectar, *Kern's*®
4 kiwifruits, peeled and chopped
1 cup ice
1 container (6-ounce) fat-free vanilla yogurt, *Dannon*®
1 tablespoon frozen limeade concentrate, *Minute Maid*®
Lime wedges (optional)
Kiwifruit wedges (optional)
Lime peel curls (optional)

1. Pour nectar into a blender. Add kiwifruits, ice, yogurt, and limeade concentrate. Cover and blend on high for 40 seconds or until smooth.

2. Pour into 2 glasses. Serve with lime wedges, kiwifruit wedges, and lime peel curls (optional).

Per serving 236 cal., 1 g total fat (0 g sat. fat), 0 mg chol., 50 mg sodium, 50 g carbo., 6 g fiber, 6 g pro.
Daily Values 3% vit. A, 284% vit. C, 21% calcium, 4% iron

Starters & Snacks

I'm a grazer from way back. One trip to the candy store was all it took to teach me that a little of a lot was much more intriguing than a lot of a little. All those flavors! This chapter follows the same principle, serving up a guilt-free menu of trendy tastes and textures that encourage you—and your guests—to nibble nutritiously instead of filling up on empty calories. It's fun food that's a whole lot lighter and a little more sophisticated. Party hearty with Roasted Portobello Crostini or dish up a dessert of refreshing Mango-Melon Bites. Balance the sweet heat of chunky Mango-and-Black Bean Salsa with the smooth elegance of Tuscan White Bean Spread. Or try salty Sweet Potato Fries as chic snacks with sauce on the side. Munchies get a gathering going, so mix them, match them—or make them a meal.

The Recipes

Chile Guacamole with Baked Tortillas

Start to Finish 35 minutes
Makes 4 cups

SUPER FOODS
Onion
Citrus
Garlic
Chile peppers
Tomatoes
Avocado

FOR BAKED TORTILLAS:

	Olive oil cooking spray, *Mazola® Pure*
3	10-inch sun-dried tomato-basil tortillas, *Mission®*
3	10-inch garden spinach-herb tortillas, *Mission®*

FOR CHILE GUACAMOLE:

2	cups frozen no-salt-added petite peas, thawed, *C&W®*
½	cup frozen chopped onions, *Ore-Ida®*
⅓	cup water
2	tablespoons lemon juice, *ReaLemon®*
1	packet (1-ounce) guacamole seasoning mix, *McCormick®*
1	teaspoon chopped garlic, *Christopher Ranch®*
1	can (7-ounce) fire-roasted diced green chiles, drained, *Ortega®*
½	cup no-salt-added diced tomatoes, *S&W®*
½	cup chopped fresh avocado
	Salt and ground black pepper
	Fresh tomatoes, chopped (optional)
	Scallions (green onions), sliced (optional)

1. For Baked Tortillas, preheat oven to 350 degrees F. Coat a baking sheet with cooking spray; set aside.

2. Using a 3-inch cookie cutter, cut tortillas into circles. Arrange on prepared baking sheet. Bake for 8 to 10 minutes or until golden. Cool chips on baking sheet on wire rack.

3. Meanwhile, for Chile Guacamole, in a medium saucepan, combine peas, onions, water, lemon juice, guacamole seasoning mix, and garlic. Cook for 10 minutes or until ingredients are soft. Remove saucepan from heat; cool.

4. Pour cooled pea mixture into a blender. Add green chiles, diced tomatoes, and avocado. Cover and blend until smooth. Season with salt and pepper. Garnish with fresh tomatoes and scallions (optional). Serve with Baked Tortillas.

Per ¼ cup dip + 4 chips 135 cal., 3 g total fat (0 g sat. fat), 3 mg chol., 398 mg sodium, 20 g carbo., 2 g fiber, 5 g pro. **Daily Values** 12% vit. A, 16% vit. C, 6% calcium, 9% iron

Caesar Artichoke Dip

Prep 10 minutes **Bake** 40 minutes
Makes 4 cups

Everybody needs one take-anywhere dip, and here's yours. Fat-free Caesar dressing, light mayonnaise, and low-fat cheese team with canned artichokes and tomatoes to make this creamy concoction a healthy hit.

SUPER FOODS
Tomatoes

Olive oil cooking spray, *Mazola® Pure*
⅔ cup fat-free Caesar salad dressing, *Girard's®*
⅓ cup light mayonnaise, *Hellmann's or Best Foods®*
⅓ cup fat-free sour cream, *Knudsen®*
⅓ cup grated Parmesan cheese, *DiGiorno®*
2 cans (15 ounces each) artichoke quarters in water, drained and chopped, *Maria®*
1 can (14.5-ounce) organic diced tomatoes with basil and garlic, drained, *Muir Glen®*
5 ounces low-fat Swiss cheese, shredded, *Alpine Lace®*
½ teaspoon hot pepper sauce, *Tabasco®*
Baked tortilla chips and/or vegetable dippers

1. Preheat oven to 350 degrees F. Coat a 1-quart baking dish with cooking spray; set aside.

2. In a medium bowl, whisk together salad dressing, mayonnaise, sour cream, and Parmesan cheese until smooth. Stir in artichokes, tomatoes, Swiss cheese, and hot pepper sauce. Transfer to prepared baking dish.

3. Bake in preheated oven for 40 to 45 minutes or until mixture is set and top is golden. Serve dip with baked tortilla chips and/or vegetable dippers.

Per ¼ cup dip + 4 baked tortilla chips 139 cal., 3 g total fat (1 g sat. fat), 7 mg chol., 501 mg sodium, 15 g carbo., 2 g fiber, 5 g pro. **Daily Values** 4% vit. A, 6% vit. C, 13% calcium, 6% iron

Mango-and-Black Bean Salsa

Prep 10 minutes **Chill** 1 hour
Makes 3½ cups

1 can (15-ounce) no-salt-added organic black beans, rinsed and drained, *Eden®*
1 can (15-ounce) petite diced tomatoes with garlic and sweet onion, drained well, *S&W®*
1½ cups refrigerated precut mango slices, drained and finely chopped, *Ready Pac®*
¼ cup chopped fresh cilantro
2 tablespoons lime juice, *ReaLime®*
Blue and/or yellow tortilla chips

SUPER FOODS
Beans
Tomatoes
Mango
Citrus

1. In a medium bowl, combine black beans, tomatoes, mango, cilantro, and lime juice. Cover with plastic wrap; chill in the refrigerator for 1 to 2 hours to allow flavors to meld. Serve with tortilla chips.

Per ¼ cup salsa + 4 tortilla chips 95 cal., 3 g total fat (0 g sat. fat), 0 mg chol., 195 mg sodium, 16 g carbo., 2 g fiber, 3 g pro. **Daily Values** 5% vit. A, 13% vit. C, 4% calcium, 6% iron

Tuscan White Bean Spread

Prep 10 minutes Chill 1 hour
Stand 30 minutes Makes 2 cups

SUPER FOODS
Beans
Yogurt
Garlic
Tomatoes

1	can (15-ounce) no-salt-added organic navy beans, rinsed and drained, *Eden®*
⅓	cup fat-free plain yogurt, *Horizon Organic®*
3	whole roasted garlic cloves, finely chopped, *Christopher Ranch®*
1	teaspoon dried Italian seasoning, *McCormick®*
¼	cup finely chopped fresh basil
2	tablespoons finely chopped oil-pack sun-dried tomatoes, *Alessi®*
	Salt and ground black pepper
	Fresh basil sprigs (optional)
	Toasted baguette-style French bread slices or water crackers

1. Place beans, yogurt, garlic, and Italian seasoning in a blender. Cover and blend until smooth.

2. Add chopped basil and tomatoes. Cover and pulse blender until combined. Season with salt and pepper. Chill in the refrigerator for 1 to 2 hours to allow flavors to meld.

3. Let spread stand at room temperature 30 minutes before serving. Garnish with basil sprigs (optional). Serve with toasted baguette slices or water crackers.

Per ¼ cup spread + 3 bread slices 107 cal., 1 g total fat (0 g sat. fat), 0 mg chol., 170 mg sodium, 19 g carbo., 5 g fiber, 6 g pro. **Daily Values** 2% vit. A, 4% vit. C, 6% calcium, 8% iron

Cucumber-Yogurt Dip with Pita Chips

Prep 20 minutes Chill 1 hour (dip)
Bake 10 minutes (chips)
Makes 2 cups

SUPER FOODS
Citrus
Whole grain breads

FOR CUCUMBER-YOGURT DIP:

1	medium cucumber
1	cup fat-free plain yogurt, *Horizon Organic®*
1	cup fat-free sour cream, *Horizon Organic®*
1	tablespoon Greek seasoning, *Spice Islands®*
1	tablespoon lemon juice, *ReaLemon®*
	Salt and ground black pepper

FOR PITA CHIPS:

	Olive oil cooking spray, *Mazola® Pure*
4	whole wheat pita bread rounds, cut into 8 wedges each, *Thomas® Sahara*
2	teaspoons Greek seasoning, *Spice Islands®*

1. For Cucumber-Yogurt Dip, cut cucumber in half lengthwise. Using a spoon, scrape out seeds. Grate cucumber into a medium bowl. Stir in yogurt, sour cream, the 1 tablespoon Greek seasoning, and lemon juice. Season with salt and pepper. Chill for 1 to 2 hours.

2. Meanwhile, for Pita Chips, preheat oven to 350 degrees F. Coat a baking sheet with cooking spray. Place pita wedges in a single layer on prepared baking sheet. Lightly coat wedges with cooking spray. Sprinkle with the 2 teaspoons Greek seasoning. Bake for 10 minutes. Cool chips on baking sheet on wire rack. Serve with Cucumber-Yogurt Dip.

Per ¼ cup dip + 4 Pita Chips 132 cal., 1 g total fat (0 g sat. fat), 3 mg chol., 326 mg sodium, 24 g carbo., 3 g fiber, 6 g pro. **Daily Values** 2% vit. A, 3% vit. C, 11% calcium, 6% iron

Roasted Portobello Crostini

Prep 20 minutes   **Chill** 1 hour
Bake 30 minutes   **Makes** 30 pieces

SUPER FOODS
Mushrooms
Garlic
Peppers

3	large portobello mushrooms
¾	cup light roasted garlic balsamic salad dressing, *Bernstein's*®
	Olive oil cooking spray, *Mazola*® *Pure*
1	loaf (12-ounce) baguette-style French bread, sliced ½ inch thick
1	cup low-fat ricotta cheese, *Precious*®
2	tablespoons light roasted garlic balsamic salad dressing, *Bernstein's*®
2	teaspoons dried Italian seasoning, *McCormick*®
	Salt and ground black pepper
½	cup roasted red bell peppers, cut into ½-inch-wide strips, *Delallo*®
	Fresh oregano leaves (optional)

1. Wipe portobello mushrooms clean with paper towels. Remove stems; use a spoon to scoop out gills. Cut mushrooms in half, then cut into ½-inch slices. Place in a large zip-top plastic bag. Add the ¾ cup salad dressing to bag with mushrooms. Squeeze air from bag and seal. Gently massage bag to blend ingredients. Chill in refrigerator for 1 to 2 hours.

2. Preheat oven to 400 degrees F. Lightly coat baking sheet with cooking spray; set aside.

3. Place bread slices on prepared baking sheet in a single layer. Lightly coat with cooking spray. Bake in preheated oven for 10 to 15 minutes or until golden. Cool bread slices on baking sheet on wire rack.

4. Coat a second baking sheet with cooking spray. Remove mushroom slices from zip-top bag; discard marinade. Place in a single layer on prepared baking sheet. Bake for 20 minutes.

5. Meanwhile, in a small bowl, stir together ricotta cheese, the 2 tablespoons balsamic dressing, and Italian seasoning. Season with salt and black pepper.

6. Spread toasted bread slices with ricotta cheese mixture. Top with a mushroom slice and cross with a bell pepper strip. Garnish with oregano leaf (optional).

Per piece 55 cal., 2 g total fat (0 g sat. fat), 3 mg chol., 209 mg sodium, 7 g carbo., 1 g fiber, 2 g pro.
Daily Values 1% vit. A, 11% vit. C, 3% calcium, 3% iron

Chicken Satay with Ginger Sauce

Prep 15 minutes   Marinate 1 hour
Broil 8 minutes   Makes 6 kabobs

Asian street vendors made strips of skewered meat dipped in peanut sauce—or satay—an easy-to-eat treat. This gingery lime-yogurt sauce makes it healthfully yours. Kids will nibble it up.

SUPER FOODS
Yogurt
Ginger
Citrus

FOR DIPPING SAUCE:
- ½   cup fat-free plain yogurt, *Horizon Organic*®
- 2   tablespoons chopped fresh cilantro
- 2   tablespoons ginger preserves, *Robertson's*®
- 2   teaspoons reduced-sodium soy sauce, *Kikkoman*®

FOR CHICKEN SATAY:
- 1½   pounds chicken tenders
- 2   tablespoons chopped fresh cilantro
- 2   tablespoons lime juice, *ReaLime*®
- 1   tablespoon salt-free Thai seasoning, *Spice Hunter*®
- 1   tablespoon reduced-sodium soy sauce, *Kikkoman*®
-   Canola oil cooking spray, *Mazola® Pure*
-   Fresh cilantro sprigs (optional)

1. For Dipping Sauce, in a small bowl, combine yogurt, 2 tablespoons chopped cilantro, preserves, and the 2 teaspoons soy sauce. Cover and refrigerate until ready to serve.

2. For Chicken Satay, place chicken tenders in a large zip-top plastic bag. For marinade, in a bowl, combine 2 tablespoons chopped cilantro, lime juice, Thai seasoning, and the 1 tablespoon soy sauce. Add to zip-top bag with chicken. Squeeze air from bag and seal. Gently massage bag to combine ingredients. Marinate in the refrigerator for 1 to 4 hours.

3. Meanwhile, soak six 8- to 10-inch wooden skewers in water for 30 minutes. Preheat the broiler. Lightly coat a baking sheet with cooking spray; set aside.

4. Remove chicken from zip-top bag; discard marinade. Drain skewers. Thread chicken on skewers. Place on prepared baking sheet.

5. Broil skewers 6 to 8 inches from heat for 4 to 5 minutes per side or until cooked through. Garnish Dipping Sauce with cilantro sprigs (optional). Serve chicken warm or at room temperature with Dipping Sauce.

Per kabob 164 cal., 2 g total fat (1 g sat. fat), 66 mg chol., 241 mg sodium, 7 g carbo., 0 g fiber, 28 g pro.
Daily Values 5% vit. A, 4% vit. C, 6% calcium, 5% iron

Sweet Potato Fries

Prep 10 minutes **Bake** 30 minutes
Makes 4 servings

2	pounds sweet potatoes, peeled
1	tablespoon canola oil, *Wesson*®
1	teaspoon pumpkin pie spice, *McCormick*®
1	tablespoon low-sodium chili seasoning, *McCormick*®
	Dipping sauces (such as fat-free mayonnaise, fat-free sour cream, and/or reduced-sodium ketchup) (optional)

SUPER FOODS
Sweet potato

1. Preheat oven to 400 degrees F. Line baking sheet with aluminum foil; set aside.

2. Cut potatoes in half lengthwise, then cut into $\frac{1}{2}$-inch-thick fries. In a large bowl, combine sweet potatoes, oil, pumpkin pie spice, and chili seasoning. Toss until potatoes are thoroughly coated. Spread fries in a single layer on prepared baking sheet.

3. Bake fries in preheated oven for 30 to 35 minutes, turning once to ensure even cooking. Serve with dipping sauces (optional).

Per serving 233 cal., 4 g total fat (0 g sat. fat), 0 mg chol., 290 mg sodium, 47 g carbo., 8 g fiber, 6 g pro.
Daily Values 591% vit. A, 10% vit. C, 8% calcium, 10% iron

Chile-Corn Muffins

Prep 10 minutes **Bake** 14 minutes
Stand 5 minutes **Makes** 36 muffins

	Canola oil cooking spray, *Mazola*® *Pure*
1	box (14.5-ounce) fat-free honey corn bread mix, *Krusteaz*®
1¼	cups buttermilk
1	can (11-ounce) Mexicorn, drained, *Green Giant*®
1	can (4-ounce) diced green chiles, drained, *Ortega*®
2	teaspoons salt-free fajita seasoning, *Spice Hunter*®

SUPER FOODS
Chile peppers

1. Preheat oven to 400 degrees F. Coat thirty-six $1\frac{1}{2}$-inch mini-muffin cups* with cooking spray; set aside.

2. In a medium bowl, stir together corn bread mix, buttermilk, Mexicorn, green chiles, and fajita seasoning until combined. Spoon batter into mini-muffin cups, filling to the rim.

3. Bake muffins in preheated oven for 14 to 16 minutes or until golden brown. Cool muffins in muffin cups on a wire rack for 5 minutes. Remove from muffin cups. Serve warm.

*NOTE: To make standard-size muffins, lightly coat eighteen to twenty $2\frac{1}{2}$-inch muffin cups with cooking spray. Spoon batter into muffin cups, filling two-thirds full. Bake in preheated oven for 16 to 18 minutes.

Per muffin 51 cal., 0 g total fat (0 g sat. fat), 0 mg chol., 214 mg sodium, 11 g carbo., 1 g fiber, 1 g pro.
Daily Values 2% vit. C, 3% calcium, 1% iron

Mango-Melon Bites

Start to Finish 15 minutes
Makes 6 servings

SUPER FOODS
Yogurt
Mango

½   cup fat-free plain yogurt, *Horizon Organic®*
¼   cup honey mustard, *French's®*
1   tablespoon salt-free lemon-pepper seasoning, *McCormick®*
     Fresh mint sprigs (optional)
1½   cups seedless red grapes
2   cups refrigerated mango chunks, *Ready Pac®*
1   package (6-ounce) ham slices, sliced in half, *Healthy Choice®*
2   cups refrigerated watermelon chunks, *Ready Pac®*

1. For dipping sauce, in a small bowl, combine yogurt, mustard, and lemon-pepper seasoning. Set aside.

2. Thread a fresh mint leaf (optional), a grape, a mango chunk, a folded half-slice ham, and a watermelon chunk on a party pick. Repeat until all ingredients are used. Serve with dipping sauce.

Per kabob 133 cal., 1 g total fat (0 g sat. fat), 14 mg chol., 323 mg sodium, 25 g carbo., 2 g fiber, 7 g pro.
Daily Values 15% vit. A, 40% vit. C, 5% calcium, 2% iron

Salads & Soups

I learned early on that the produce aisle is the widest for a reason—it's home to the foods everyone should eat the most of. Nutritionists recommend 4 to 5 servings of fruits and vegetables a day. A big leafy salad and a side of soup should make quick work of that … and treat the taste buds too. This chapter is filled with old faithfuls newly enlightened: chicken salad with a tropical twist, tuna salad spiced up with white beans, California-style gazpacho with sunshiny vegetables. Even non-meat eaters can load up on heart-healthy Quinoa Salad and Pumpkin-and-Pear Soup with Maple Cream.

The Recipes

Greek Turkey Salad

Start to Finish 20 minutes
Makes 6 servings

SUPER FOODS
Citrus
Tomatoes
Onion
Garlic

Olive oil cooking spray, *Mazola® Pure*
1 package (1.25-pound) turkey breast strips, *Jennie-O®*
2 tablespoons lemon juice, *ReaLemon®*
1 tablespoon Greek seasoning, *Spice Islands®*
Salt and ground black pepper
12 cups (about 20 ounces) packaged chopped romaine lettuce, *Fresh Express®*
1 cucumber, seeded and chopped
2 medium tomatoes, cut up
½ medium red onion, thinly sliced
½ cup pitted kalamata olives, drained, *Mezzetta®*
⅓ cup crumbled feta cheese, *Athenos®*
¾ cup light roasted garlic balsamic salad dressing, *Bernstein's®*
¼ cup fresh oregano leaves

1. Coat a large nonstick skillet with cooking spray. Heat skillet over medium-high heat. Add turkey, lemon juice, and Greek seasoning. Cook and stir for 5 to 7 minutes or until turkey is cooked through. Season with salt and pepper. Set aside to cool.

2. In a large salad bowl, combine romaine, cucumber, tomatoes, red onion, olives, and feta cheese. Toss with salad dressing.

3. Top with turkey strips. Garnish with oregano leaves.

SERVING IDEAS: Serve with warm or toasted whole wheat pita bread.

Per serving 231 cal., 8 g total fat (2 g sat. fat), 66 mg chol., 824 mg sodium, 12 g carbo., 4 g fiber, 27 g pro.
Daily Values 140% vit. A, 62% vit. C, 12% calcium, 14% iron

Chicken-Tarragon
Salad

Start to Finish 15 minutes
Makes 4 servings

Tarragon gives this rendition of a Waldorf salad a licorice lift. Fiber-filled grapes and potassium-packed celery stand in for apples, while walnuts add satisfying crunch. Serve for a light dinner or a refreshing lunch.

SUPER FOODS
Yogurt
Walnuts
Onion

$\frac{1}{2}$	cup fat-free mayonnaise, *Hellmann's® or Best Foods®*
$\frac{1}{4}$	cup fat-free plain yogurt, *Horizon Organic®*
2	teaspoons finely chopped fresh tarragon
1	teaspoon poppy seeds, *McCormick®*
2	pouches (7 ounces each) chunk chicken breast meat, rinsed and drained, *Tyson®*
1	cup seedless red grapes, cut in half
2	ribs celery, chopped
$\frac{1}{4}$	cup chopped walnuts, *Planters®*
6	cups packaged spring mix lettuce, *Ready Pac®*
$\frac{1}{4}$	cup chopped red onion

1. For dressing, in a small bowl, whisk together mayonnaise, yogurt, 1 teaspoon of the tarragon, and poppy seeds; set aside.

2. In a medium bowl, combine chicken, grapes, and celery. Set aside 1 tablespoon of the walnuts. Add remaining walnuts to chicken. Pour $\frac{1}{2}$ cup of the dressing over mixture and stir to combine.

3. In a large bowl, toss lettuce with the remaining $\frac{1}{4}$ cup dressing. Divide mixture among 4 chilled plates. Divide chicken mixture among plates. Sprinkle each plate with some of the remaining 1 teaspoon tarragon, the reserved walnuts, and the onion.

Per serving 232 cal., 7 g total fat (1 g sat. fat), 53 mg chol., 571 mg sodium, 17 g carbo., 2 g fiber, 27 g pro.
Daily Values 18% vit. A, 18% vit. C, 9% calcium, 5% iron

Tropical Chicken Salad

Prep 15 minutes **Grill** 8 minutes
Makes 4 servings

SUPER FOODS

Olive oil
Pineapple
Yogurt
Citrus
Mango
Strawberries
Avocado

4	boneless, skinless chicken breast halves
2	teaspoons extra-virgin olive oil, *Bertolli*®
	Refrigerated pineapple chunks, *Del Monte*®
$\frac{1}{3}$	cup fat-free plain yogurt, *Horizon Organic*®
1	tablespoon orange juice concentrate, *Minute Maid*®
4	cups packaged chopped romaine lettuce, *Ready Pac*®
1	cup refrigerated mango chunks, drained, *Del Monte*®
8	whole strawberries
1	avocado, sliced

1. Set up grill for direct cooking over high heat. Brush both sides of chicken breast halves with olive oil; set aside.

2. Oil grate when ready to start cooking. Place chicken on hot oiled grill. Cook for 4 to 6 minutes per side or until chicken is no longer pink (170 degrees F).

3. For dressing, drain pineapple, reserving $\frac{1}{3}$ cup juice. Measure 1 cup pineapple chunks; set aside. Refrigerate remaining juice and pineapple for another use. In a small bowl, whisk together the $\frac{1}{3}$ cup reserved pineapple juice, yogurt, and orange juice concentrate. Set aside.

4. On a large platter, arrange romaine, chicken, pineapple chunks, mango chunks, strawberries, and avocado slices. Serve with dressing.

Per serving 383 cal., 11 g total fat (2 g sat. fat), 83 mg chol., 113 mg sodium, 29 g carbo., 5 g fiber, 36 g pro.
Daily Values 75% vit. A, 226% vit. C, 9% calcium, 15% iron

Chicken and Baby Spinach with Raspberry-Balsamic Vinaigrette

Start to Finish 15 minutes
Makes 4 servings

1 ½ cups fresh raspberries
½ cup light balsamic vinaigrette, *Newman's Own®*
¾ teaspoon sugar
8 cups packaged baby spinach, *Ready Pac®*
1 cup sliced cucumber
⅓ cup thinly sliced red onion
1 ⅓ cups purchased cooked chicken breast cut into strips, *Tyson®*
¼ cup crumbled feta cheese, *Athenos®*
¼ cup chopped pecans, *Blue Diamond®*
   Ground black pepper, *McCormick®*

SUPER FOODS
Raspberries
Spinach
Onion
Pecans

1. For dressing, place ½ cup of the raspberries, salad dressing, and sugar in a blender. Cover and blend until smooth; set aside.

2. In a large bowl, toss together the remaining 1 cup raspberries, spinach, cucumber, onion, and half of the dressing.

3. Divide mixture among 4 chilled plates. Toss chicken strips with 2 tablespoons of the dressing. Divide among the plates. Top with feta cheese and pecans. Season with pepper. Pass remaining dressing.

Per serving 237 cal., 13 g total fat (3 g sat. fat), 51 mg chol., 660 mg sodium, 11 g carbo., 6 g fiber, 20 g pro.
Daily Values 115% vit. A, 46% vit. C, 13% calcium, 16% iron

Mexican Chef's Salad

Start to Finish 20 minutes
Makes 4 servings

SUPER FOODS
Tomatoes
Beans
Onions

Olive oil cooking spray, *Mazola® Pure*
1   pound ground uncooked turkey breast
¾   cup water
1   packet (1.25-ounce) low-sodium chili seasoning mix, *McCormick®*
½   cup cilantro-flavored salsa, *Pace®*
½   cup fat-free Thousand Island salad dressing, *Kraft®*
8   cups packaged chopped romaine lettuce, *Fresh Express®*
1⅓   cups no-salt-added organic kidney beans, rinsed and drained, *Eden®*
1   cup frozen organic whole-kernel corn, thawed, *Cascadian Farm®*
2   tomatoes, cut into eighths
2   scallions (green onions), sliced
¼   cup jalapeño smokehouse almonds, chopped, *Blue Diamond®* (optional)

1. Coat a nonstick skillet with cooking spray. Add turkey; cook and stir until turkey is brown. Drain; stir in water and chili seasoning mix. Bring to a boil; reduce heat. Simmer for 5 minutes, stirring occasionally. Remove from heat; set aside.

2. For dressing, in a small bowl, stir together salsa and salad dressing.

3. In a large bowl, toss romaine with half of the dressing. Divide among 4 chilled plates. Divide turkey, kidney beans, corn, and tomatoes among plates. Sprinkle with scallions. Garnish with almonds (optional). Serve with remaining dressing.

Per serving 337 cal., 3 g total fat (1 g sat. fat), 45 mg chol., 806 mg sodium, 43 g carbo., 14 g fiber, 35 g pro.
Daily Values 165% vit. A, 65% vit. C, 10% calcium, 26% iron

Cajun Salmon Salad

Prep 15 minutes **Grill** 8 minutes
Makes 4 servings

1	**1-pound fresh or frozen salmon fillet**
1	**tablespoon extra-virgin olive oil, *Bertolli*®**
2	**tablespoons Cajun seasoning, *McCormick*®**
½	**cup fat-free Thousand Island salad dressing, *Kraft*®**
1	**teaspoon hot pepper sauce, *Tabasco*®**
¼	**teaspoon Cajun seasoning, *McCormick*®**
4	**cups packaged lettuce mix, *Ready Pac*®**
1	**cup cooked brown rice, *Uncle Ben's*® *Ready Rice***
1	**cup no-salt-added organic kidney beans, rinsed and drained, *Eden*®**
½	**cup chopped roasted red bell peppers, *Delallo*®**

SUPER FOODS
Salmon
Olive oil
Whole grains
Beans
Peppers

1. Thaw fish, if frozen. Set up grill for direct cooking over medium-high heat. Rinse fish under cold water and pat dry with paper towels. Remove bones. Brush both sides of fish with olive oil and sprinkle with the 2 tablespoons Cajun seasoning; set aside.

2. Oil grate when ready to start grilling. Place fish on hot oiled grill. Cook for 4 to 6 minutes per side or until fish flakes easily when tested with a fork. Do not overcook.

3. For dressing, in a small bowl, combine salad dressing, hot pepper sauce, and the ¼ teaspoon Cajun seasoning.

4. Divide lettuce among 4 chilled plates. Top each plate with ¼ cup rice, ¼ cup beans, 2 tablespoons bell peppers, and one-quarter of the fish. Serve with dressing.

Per serving 407 cal., 17 g total fat (3 g sat. fat), 66 mg chol., 657 mg sodium, 34 g carbo., 8 g fiber, 29 g pro.
Daily Values 7% vit. A, 96% vit. C, 7% calcium, 16% iron

Quinoa Salad

Start to Finish 30 minutes
Makes 6 servings

SUPER FOODS
Quinoa
Peppers
Onions
Almonds

2   cups organic chicken or vegetable broth, *Swanson*®
1   cup quinoa
1   cup seeded and chopped cucumber
½   cup chopped roasted red bell peppers, *Delallo*®
½   cup crumbled feta cheese, *Athens*®
¼   cup finely chopped flat-leaf parsley
2   scallions (green onions), sliced
3   tablespoons slivered almonds, toasted, *Planters*®
1   tablespoon fines herbes, *Spice Islands*®
9   cups Bibb lettuce leaves, torn
¼   cup light roasted garlic and balsamic salad dressing, *Bernstein's*®

1. In a medium saucepan, combine chicken broth and quinoa. Bring to a boil; reduce heat. Cover and simmer for 10 to 15 minutes or until liquid is absorbed. Spread quinoa on a baking sheet; cool.

2. In a large bowl, combine cooled quinoa, cucumber, roasted peppers, feta cheese, parsley, scallions, almonds, and fines herbes. Toss to mix.

3. Toss lettuce with quinoa mixture; divide among 6 chilled salad plates. Drizzle with salad dressing.

Per serving 204 cal., 8 g total fat (2 g sat. fat), 12 mg chol., 636 mg sodium, 26 g carbo., 4 g fiber, 8 g pro.
Daily Values 23% vit. A, 73% vit. C, 14% calcium, 22% iron

Tuna and Spicy White Bean Salad

Start to Finish 10 minutes
Makes 6 servings

SUPER FOODS
Beans
Tuna
Yogurt
Citrus

1   can (15-ounce) no-salt-added organic navy beans, rinsed and drained, *Eden*®
2   cans (6 ounces each) albacore tuna in water, drained
1   cup frozen whole-kernel corn, thawed, *Birds Eye*®
1   cup peeled, seeded, and chopped cucumber
½   cup fat-free plain yogurt, *Horizon Organic*®
¼   cup finely chopped flat-leaf parsley
1   jalapeño chile pepper,* chopped
2   tablespoons lemon juice, *ReaLemon*®
  Salt and ground black pepper
9   cups packaged spring salad mix, *Ready Pac*®

1. In a large bowl, toss together beans, tuna, corn, cucumber, yogurt, parsley, chile pepper, and lemon juice. Season with salt and black pepper.

2. Divide salad mix among 6 chilled plates. Divide tuna mixture among the plates.

*NOTE: Because chile peppers contain volatile oils that can burn your skin and eyes, avoid direct contact with them as much as possible. When working with chile peppers, wear plastic or rubber gloves. If your bare hands do touch the peppers, wash your hands and nails well with soap and warm water.

Per serving 179 cal., 2 g total fat (1 g sat. fat), 24 mg chol., 300 mg sodium, 20 g carbo., 7 g fiber, 21 g pro.
Daily Values 22% vit. A, 22% vit. C, 11% calcium, 13% iron

Chicken-Corn Chowder

Start to Finish 30 minutes
Makes 6 servings

4	cups organic chicken broth, *Swanson®*
2	ribs celery, chopped
1	cup frozen chopped onions, *Ore-Ida®*
½	cup frozen chopped green bell peppers, *Pictsweet®*
1	teaspoon crushed garlic, *Christopher Ranch®*
	Olive oil cooking spray, *Mazola® Pure*
1	pound boneless, skinless chicken breast halves, cut into bite-size pieces
2	cups frozen organic whole-kernel corn, *Cascadian Farm®*
1	baked potato,* cut into bite-size pieces
1	cup reconstituted nonfat dry milk powder, *Carnation®*
⅓	cup chopped roasted red bell peppers, *Delallo®*
2	teaspoons salt-free chicken seasoning, *McCormick®*
	Salt and ground black pepper
	Fresh parsley, chopped (optional)

SUPER FOODS
Onions
Peppers
Garlic

1. In a microwave-safe bowl, combine ½ cup of the chicken broth, celery, onions, green peppers, and garlic. Cover and cook on high setting (100% power) for 5 minutes; set aside.

2. Coat the bottom of a large pot with cooking spray; heat over medium-high heat. Add chicken; cook and stir for 5 to 7 minutes or until chicken is no longer pink.

3. Add celery mixture, the remaining 3½ cups broth, corn, potato, milk, red peppers, and chicken seasoning. Bring to boil; reduce heat. Simmer for 10 to 15 minutes or until desired consistency, stirring occasionally. Season with salt and black pepper. Garnish with parsley (optional).

*NOTE: To bake potato, preheat oven to 425 degrees F. Prick potato with a fork. Bake in preheated oven for 40 to 60 minutes or until tender. (Or microwave on high setting [100% power] for 4 to 6 minutes or until tender.)

Per serving 284 cal., 3 g total fat (1 g sat. fat), 64 mg chol., 878 mg sodium, 31 g carbo., 3 g fiber, 33 g pro.
Daily Values 4% vit. A, 54% vit. C, 28% calcium, 10% iron

Enchilada Soup

Start to Finish 20 minutes
Makes 6 servings

SUPER FOODS
Onion
Tomato
Chile peppers
Garlic

Olive oil cooking spray, *Mazola® Pure*
1 ¼ pounds ground uncooked turkey breast
1 cup chopped red onion
4 cups organic chicken broth, *Swanson®*
1 cup reduced-fat cheese dip, *Tostitos®*
¾ cup tomato puree, *Muir Glen®*
1 can (4-ounce) diced green chiles, drained, *La Victoria®*
1 tablespoon enchilada sauce mix, *Lawry's®*
1 teaspoon crushed garlic, *Christopher Ranch®*
¼ cup finely chopped fresh cilantro
Jalapeño chile peppers, sliced (see note, page 62) (optional)
¾ cup baked blue corn chips, *Guiltless® Gourmet*

1. Coat the bottom of a large pot with cooking spray; heat over medium-high heat. Add turkey and onion. Cook and stir until turkey is no longer pink, stirring often to break up large clumps.

2. Add broth, cheese dip, tomato puree, chiles, enchilada sauce mix, and garlic. Bring to a boil; reduce heat. Simmer for 10 minutes. Stir in cilantro. Garnish with jalapeño peppers (optional). Serve with corn chips.

Per serving 227 cal., 5 g total fat (2 g sat. fat), 40 mg chol., 619 mg sodium, 17 g carbo., 2 g fiber, 28 g pro.
Daily Values 5% vit. A, 22% vit. C, 8% calcium, 11% iron

Gazpacho Monterey

Prep 15 minutes **Chill** 1 hour
Makes 6 servings

SUPER FOODS
Tomatoes
Peppers
Citrus
Garlic
Chile peppers

1 can (28-ounce) whole peeled organic tomatoes in juice, *Muir Glen®*
1 bag (16-ounce) frozen pepper stir-fry, *Birds Eye®*
1 cup organic chicken broth, *Swanson®*
1 cup orange juice, *Minute Maid®*
4 cloves whole peeled garlic, *Christopher Ranch®*
1 jalapeño chile pepper, seeds removed and chopped (see note, page 62)
1 slice whole grain bread, torn into pieces, *Oroweat® Health Nut*
Salt and ground black pepper
3 tablespoons fresh cilantro leaves
Lime wedges (optional)

1. Combine tomatoes, stir-fry peppers, chicken broth, orange juice, garlic, chile pepper, and bread in a blender (work in batches, if necessary). Cover and blend until smooth. Transfer to a large bowl. Season with salt and black pepper. Cover and chill for 1 hour.

2. To serve, top soup with cilantro. Serve with lime wedges (optional).

Per serving 82 cal., 0 g total fat (0 g sat. fat), 0 mg chol., 408 mg sodium, 17 g carbo., 3 g fiber, 3 g pro.
Daily Values 15% vit. A, 85% vit. C, 5% calcium, 10% iron

Pumpkin-and-Pear Soup with Maple Cream

Start to Finish 45 minutes
Makes 6 servings

4	cups organic chicken or vegetable broth, *Swanson®*
1	cup frozen chopped onions, *Ore-Ida®*
2	ribs celery, chopped
1	cup frozen sliced carrots, *C&W®*
1	teaspoon crushed garlic, *Christopher Ranch®*
2	cans (15 ounces each) light sliced pears, *Del Monte®*
1	can (15-ounce) pumpkin, *Libby's®*
1½	teaspoons pumpkin pie spice, *McCormick®*
1½	teaspoons ground cumin, *McCormick®*
½	cup light sour cream, *Horizon Organic®*
1	tablespoon pure maple syrup, *Maple Grove Farms®*
¼	teaspoon pumpkin pie spice, *McCormick®*
	Fresh chives, chopped (optional)
	Baked Pita Chips (optional)

SUPER FOODS
Onions
Carrots
Garlic
Pumpkin

1. In a medium microwave-safe bowl, combine 1 cup of the chicken broth, onions, celery, carrots, and garlic. Cover and cook on high setting (100% power) for 8 minutes.

2. In a large pot, combine onion mixture, the remaining broth, pears, pumpkin, the 1½ teaspoons pumpkin pie spice, and cumin. Bring to a boil; reduce heat. Simmer for 20 minutes.

3. Transfer some of the mixture to a blender, filling it only half full. Cover blender and place a clean towel on top. Blend until smooth. (Or use a handheld blender.) Transfer to a large bowl. Repeat until all of the mixture has been blended.

4. For Maple Cream, in a small bowl, combine sour cream, maple syrup, and the ¼ teaspoon pumpkin pie spice, stirring until smooth. To serve, ladle soup into 6 bowls. Drizzle with some of the Maple Cream. Garnish with chives (optional). Serve with Baked Pita Chips (optional).

Per serving 178 cal., 4 g total fat (2 g sat. fat), 21 mg chol., 707 mg sodium, 30 g carbo., 4 g fiber, 7 g pro.
Daily Values 271% vit. A, 12% vit. C, 7% calcium, 11% iron

BAKED PITA CHIPS: Preheat oven to 350 degrees F. Coat baking sheet with olive oil cooking spray (*Mazola® Pure*); set aside. Cut 4 whole grain pita bread rounds (*Thomas'® Sahara*) into 8 wedges each. Place pita wedges in a single layer on prepared baking sheet. Lightly coat wedges with olive oil cooking spray. Bake in preheated oven for 10 minutes. Cool chips on baking sheet on a wire rack.

Pastas & Pizzas

Wolfgang Puck made me think of pizza in a whole new way. Instead of greasy pepperonis and strings of cheese, he served smoked salmon with cream sauce topped with capers and dill—on a crust. If pizza could be made light and healthy, I knew anything could—creamy Alfredo sauces, olive oil-soaked pestos, rich, meaty sauces. This chapter pays tribute to a diversity of foods and flavors that are authentically Italian—and authentically healthy. The secret is in the sauce, so go light and white with Angel Hair Pasta with Spicy Clam Sauce or robust and red with Spaghetti Bolognese. Vegetable lovers can have their pick of a Garden Vegetable Calzone or Sherried Mushrooms-and-Onion Penne. And while Creole Shrimp Pizza might seem indulgent, low-fat cheese makes it surprisingly heart smart. In Italy, food is love, so boil some noodles, toss a salad, bake a pizza, and spread it around.

The Recipes

Spaghetti Bolognese

Start to Finish 25 minutes
Makes 8 servings

SUPER FOODS

Carrots
Onions
Garlic
Mushrooms

1	box (16-ounce) spaghetti, *Barilla® Plus*
½	cup chopped carrots
½	cup chopped celery
2	tablespoons water
	Olive oil cooking spray, *Mazola® Pure*
1¼	pounds ground uncooked turkey breast
1	cup frozen chopped onions, *Ore-Ida®*
1	teaspoon crushed garlic, *Christopher Ranch®*
1	jar (25.5-ounce) organic portobello mushroom pasta sauce, *Muir Glen®*
1	cup red wine, Merlot
1	cup organic chicken broth, *Swanson®*
¼	cup fat-free evaporated milk, *Carnation®*
	Celery stalks (optional)

1. In a large pot of boiling salted water, cook pasta according to package directions. Drain well; return pasta to hot pot. Cover; keep warm.

2. Meanwhile, in a microwave-safe bowl, combine carrots, chopped celery, and water. Cover and microwave on high setting (100% power) for 8 to 10 minutes or until softened; set aside.

3. Coat a large skillet with cooking spray. Add ground turkey, onions, and garlic. Cook and stir until turkey is no longer pink, stirring often to break up large clumps.

4. Add cooked carrots and celery, pasta sauce, wine, and chicken broth to skillet. Bring to a boil; reduce heat. Simmer for 5 to 10 minutes or until sauce thickens. Stir in evaporated milk. Serve over hot cooked pasta. Garnish with celery stalks (optional).

Per serving 386 cal., 4 g total fat (1 g sat. fat), 39 mg chol., 527 mg sodium, 48 g carbo., 6 g fiber, 31 g pro.
Daily Values 38% vit. A, 9% vit. C, 8% calcium, 21% iron

Spaghetti with Minted Pesto

Start to Finish 25 minutes
Makes 6 servings

For a fresh approach to pesto, replace some of the verdant basil with sweeter mint. To save time—and add punch to your pesto—make it and refrigerate it the day before so the flavors can mingle.

12	ounces spaghetti, *Barilla® Plus*
1	cup no-salt-added frozen petite peas, *C&W®*
1	tablespoon water
4	cups packed fresh basil leaves
1½	cups packed fresh mint leaves
2	tablespoons chopped walnuts, *Blue Diamond®*
5	whole roasted garlic cloves, *Christopher Ranch®*
¾	cup organic chicken broth, *Swanson®*
1	tablespoon extra-virgin olive oil, *Bertolli®*
	Salt and ground black pepper

1. In a large pot of boiling salted water, cook pasta according to package directions. Drain well; return pasta to hot pot. Cover; keep warm.

2. Meanwhile, in a microwave-safe bowl, combine peas and water. Cover and microwave on high setting (100% power) for 5 minutes. Drain; cool completely. Set aside a few peas for garnish (optional).

3. In a food processor, combine basil and mint. Cover; pulse until finely chopped. Add walnuts and garlic. Cover and pulse until thoroughly chopped and combined. With food processor running, slowly pour in chicken broth and olive oil. Add cooled peas. Cover and process until smooth. Season with salt and pepper.

4. Toss mixture with hot cooked pasta. Garnish with the reserved peas (optional).

SERVING IDEAS: Top pasta with grilled chicken or a grilled salmon fillet.

Per serving 272 cal., 5 g total fat (0 g sat. fat), 0 mg chol., 272 mg sodium, 44 g carbo., 6 g fiber, 13 g pro.
Daily Values 40% vit. A, 39% vit. C, 10% calcium, 38% iron

Angel Hair with Creamy Rosa Sauce

Start to Finish 25 minutes
Makes 6 servings

SUPER FOODS

Tomatoes

12	ounces angel hair pasta, *Barilla® Plus*
1	can (12-ounce) fat-free evaporated milk, *Carnation®*
1	tablespoon all-purpose flour
2	cups organic spicy tomato pasta sauce, *Muir Glen®*
2	ounces prosciutto, finely chopped
¼	cup finely chopped fresh basil
1	tablespoon sherry vinegar

1. In a large pot of boiling salted water, cook pasta according to package directions. Drain; return pasta to hot pot. Cover; keep warm.

2. Meanwhile, in a large saucepan, combine evaporated milk and flour. Bring to a simmer over medium-high heat until mixture thickens, whisking constantly. Once thickened and bubbling, cook for 1 minute.

3. Stir in pasta sauce, prosciutto, chopped basil, and vinegar. Bring to a boil; reduce heat. Simmer for 10 minutes. Toss with hot cooked pasta. Garnish with fresh basil leaves (optional).

Per serving 332 cal., 5 g total fat (1 g sat. fat), 7 mg chol., 652 mg sodium, 47 g carbo., 5 g fiber, 16 g pro.
Daily Values 13% vit. A, 6% vit. C, 23% calcium, 15% iron

Angel Hair with Spicy Clam Sauce

Start to Finish 25 minutes
Makes 6 servings

SUPER FOODS

Onions
Garlic
Tomatoes
Chile peppers

12	ounces angel hair pasta, *Barilla® Plus*
1	cup frozen chopped onions, *Ore-Ida®*
1	cup Chardonnay or other white wine
1	teaspoon crushed garlic, *Christopher Ranch®*
1	jar (25.5-ounce) organic spicy tomato pasta sauce, *Muir Glen®*
2	cans (6.5 ounces each) chopped clams, drained, *Snow's®*
¼	teaspoon red pepper flakes, *McCormick®*

1. In a large pot, cook pasta according to package directions. Drain; return pasta to hot pot. Cover; keep warm. In a large nonstick skillet, combine onions, wine, and garlic. Bring to slow boil over medium-high heat. Cook until liquid is reduced to ¼ cup. Stir in pasta sauce, clams, and pepper flakes. Bring to a boil. Simmer for 5 to 10 minutes or until sauce has thickened. Serve with pasta. Garnish with oregano (optional).

Per serving 417 cal., 7 g total fat (1 g sat. fat), 41 mg chol., 611 mg sodium, 53 g carbo., 6 g fiber, 29 g pro.
Daily Values 17% vit. A, 31% vit. C, 18% calcium, 112% iron

Sun-Dried Tomato Primavera

Start to Finish 35 minutes
Makes 6 servings

12	ounces rotini pasta, *Barilla® Plus*
½	pound asparagus, trimmed and cut into 1-inch pieces
1	zucchini, halved lengthwise and sliced
1	yellow summer squash, halved lengthwise and sliced
2	teaspoons extra-virgin olive oil, *Bertolli®*
1	jar (25.5-ounce) organic Italian herb pasta sauce, *Muir Glen®*
1½	cups frozen bell pepper strips, *C&W®*
¼	cup oil-pack sun-dried tomatoes, drained and chopped, *Alessi®*
½	cup organic chicken broth, *Swanson®*
¼	cup finely chopped fresh mint
¼	cup finely chopped fresh basil
1	tablespoon balsamic vinegar
	Salt and ground black pepper
	Shredded Parmesan cheese, *Kraft®* (optional)

SUPER FOODS

Olive oil
Peppers
Tomatoes

1. Preheat oven to 400 degrees F. In a large pot of boiling salted water, cook pasta according to package directions. Drain well; return pasta to hot pot. Cover; keep warm.

2. In a medium bowl, combine asparagus, zucchini, yellow summer squash, and olive oil, tossing to coat vegetables. Spread in a single layer on a baking sheet. Roast in preheated oven for 10 minutes; set aside.

3. In a large skillet, combine pasta sauce, bell peppers, and tomatoes. Bring to a low boil. Stir in roasted vegetables, chicken broth, mint, basil, and vinegar; reduce heat. Simmer about 10 minutes or until thickened. Season to taste with salt and black pepper. Serve over hot cooked pasta. Sprinkle with Parmesan cheese (optional).

Per serving 295 cal., 4 g total fat (0 g sat. fat), 0 mg chol., 432 mg sodium, 55 g carbo., 6 g fiber, 14 g pro.
Daily Values 53% vit. A, 70% vit. C, 8% calcium, 25% iron

Penne with Asparagus and Peppers

Start to Finish 25 minutes
Makes 6 servings

SUPER FOODS

Onions

Peppers

Garlic

Dazzling colors, good carbs, and megavitamin veggies in one trattoria-type dish—what more could you ask for? Roasting the asparagus brings out an earthy note that contrasts nicely with the bell peppers.

12	ounces penne pasta, *Barilla® Plus*
1	package (9-ounce) frozen cut organic asparagus, *Cascadian Farm®*
¾	cup organic chicken broth, *Swanson®*
½	cup frozen chopped onions, *Ore-Ida®*
½	cup roasted red bell peppers, cut into ½-inch strips, *Delallo®*
½	cup roasted yellow bell peppers, cut into ½-inch strips, *Delallo®*
1	teaspoon dried Italian seasoning, *McCormick®*
1	teaspoon crushed garlic, *Christopher Ranch®*
2	tablespoons finely chopped fresh flat-leaf parsley
1	tablespoon balsamic vinegar

1. In a large pot of boiling salted water, cook pasta according to package directions. Drain well; return pasta to hot pot. Cover; keep warm.

2. In a large skillet, combine asparagus, chicken broth, onions, peppers, Italian seasoning, and garlic. Bring to a boil; reduce heat. Simmer for 8 to 10 minutes or until liquid is reduced to ¼ cup. Stir in parsley and vinegar. Toss with hot cooked pasta.

Per serving 244 cal., 2 g total fat (0 g sat. fat), 7 mg chol., 158 mg sodium, 44 g carbo., 5 g fiber, 14 g pro.
Daily Values 11% vit. A, 163% vit. C, 4% calcium, 16% iron

Sherried Mushrooms-and-Onion Penne

Start to Finish 25 minutes
Makes 6 servings

12	ounces penne pasta, *Barilla® Plus*
1	tablespoon extra-virgin olive oil, *Bertolli®*
1	red onion, quartered and thinly sliced
2	packages (8 ounces each) sliced fresh mushrooms
¼	cup sherry, *Christian Brothers®*
2	teaspoons fines herbes, *Spice Islands®*
½	cup reduced-sodium beef broth, *Swanson®*
⅓	cup light sour cream, *Horizon Organic®*
	Fresh parsley, finely chopped (optional)

SUPER FOODS

Olive oil
Onion
Mushrooms

1. In a large pot of boiling salted water, cook pasta according to package directions. Drain well; return pasta to hot pot. Cover; keep warm.

2. In a large nonstick skillet, heat oil over medium-high heat. Add onion; cook and stir for 8 to 10 minutes or until cooked down and wilted. Add mushrooms; cook and stir for 10 minutes more. Stir in sherry and fines herbes. Cook until liquid is evaporated.

3. In a small bowl, combine beef broth and sour cream. Stir into mixture in skillet; cook for 4 to 5 minutes or until heated through.

4. Toss mixture with hot cooked pasta. Garnish with parsley (optional).

Per serving 281 cal., 6 g total fat (1 g sat. fat), 4 mg chol., 74 mg sodium, 44 g carbo., 5 g fiber, 13 g pro.
Daily Values 1% vit. A, 3% vit. C, 4% calcium, 13% iron

Chicken with Roasted Garlic Pizza

Prep 20 minutes **Bake** 12 minutes
Makes 4 servings

SUPER FOODS

Tomatoes

Garlic

Olive oil cooking spray, *Mazola® Pure*

1 package (6.5-ounce) pizza crust mix, *Betty Crocker®*

2 teaspoons salt-free chicken seasoning, *McCormick®*

½ cup hot water

¾ cup organic four cheese pasta sauce, *Muir Glen®*

¼ cup fat-free Caesar salad dressing, *Girard's®*

½ cup shredded low-fat mozzarella cheese, *Precious®*

1 tablespoon thinly sliced roasted garlic cloves, *Christopher Ranch®*

1 package (7-ounce) chunk chicken breast meat, rinsed and drained, *Tyson®*

1 tablespoon finely chopped flat-leaf parsley

1. Preheat oven to 450 degrees F. Lightly coat a baking sheet with cooking spray; set aside.

2. In a medium bowl, combine pizza crust mix and chicken seasoning. Stir in hot water until mixture is well moistened. Beat 20 times to form dough. Cover and let rest for 5 to 10 minutes.

3. Meanwhile, in a small bowl, stir together pasta sauce and salad dressing; set aside.

4. Using floured fingers, press dough into a 12-inch circle on prepared baking sheet. Top with pasta sauce mixture, leaving a 1-inch border. Sprinkle with mozzarella cheese and garlic. Add chicken and parsley.

5. Bake pizza in preheated oven for 12 to 17 minutes or until crust is golden brown.

Per serving 319 cal., 7 g total fat (2 g sat. fat), 35 mg chol., 914 mg sodium, 40 g carbo., 2 g fiber, 22 g pro.
Daily Values 6% vit. A, 8% vit. C, 14% calcium, 12% iron

Southwest Chicken Pizza

Prep 20 minutes **Bake** 15 minutes
Makes 4 servings

	Olive oil cooking spray, *Mazola® Pure*
1	package (6.5-ounce) pizza crust mix, *Betty Crocker®*
¼	cup organic black beans, rinsed, drained, and smashed, *Eden®*
½	cup hot water
½	cup tequila-and lime-flavored salsa, *Newman's Own®*
⅓	cup Mexicorn, drained, *Green Giant®*
¼	cup shredded fat-free Monterey Jack cheese with peppers, *Lifetime®*
2	tablespoons shredded reduced-fat Mexican cheese blend, *Sargento®*
1	cup premium chunk chicken breast, rinsed and drained, *Tyson®*
2	tablespoons finely chopped fresh cilantro
2	tablespoons finely chopped red onion

SUPER FOODS

Beans
Tomatoes
Onion

1. Preheat oven to 450 degrees F. Coat a baking sheet with cooking spray; set aside.

2. In a medium bowl, combine pizza crust mix and beans. Stir in hot water until mixture is well moistened. Beat 20 times to form dough. Cover and let rest for 5 to 10 minutes.

3. Using floured fingers, press dough into a 12-inch circle on prepared baking sheet. Spread salsa evenly over dough, leaving a 1-inch border. Top with Mexicorn, Monterey Jack cheese, Mexican cheese blend, chicken, cilantro, and onion.

4. Bake pizza in preheated oven for 15 to 17 minutes or until crust is golden brown.

Per serving 273 cal., 3 g total fat (0 g sat. fat), 22 mg chol., 893 mg sodium, 42 g carbo., 2 g fiber, 18 g pro.
Daily Values 8% vit. A, 3% vit. C, 10% calcium, 15% iron

BBQ Turkey Pizza

Prep 20 minutes **Bake** 12 minutes
Makes 4 servings

SUPER FOODS
Onion

Olive oil cooking spray, *Mazola® Pure*
1 package (6.5-ounce) pizza crust mix, *Betty Crocker®*
2 tablespoons cornmeal
½ cup hot water
1 cup diced cooked turkey breast
⅓ cup barbecue sauce, *Sweet Baby Ray's®*
2 tablespoons chopped red onion
¼ cup shredded low-fat mozzarella cheese, *Precious®*
1 tablespoon shredded Gouda cheese
2 tablespoons finely chopped fresh cilantro

1. Preheat oven to 450 degrees F. Coat a large baking sheet with cooking spray; set aside.

2. In a medium bowl, combine pizza crust mix and cornmeal. Stir in hot water until mixture is well moistened. Beat 20 times to form dough. Cover and let rest for 5 to 10 minutes.

3. Meanwhile, coat a small saucepan with cooking spray; heat over medium-high heat. Add turkey and 1 tablespoon of the barbecue sauce. Cook and stir for 4 to 6 minutes. Remove from heat; set aside.

4. Divide dough into 4 portions. Using floured fingers, press each dough portion into a 5-inch circle on prepared baking sheet. Spread the remaining barbecue sauce evenly over dough rounds, leaving a ½-inch border. Top with turkey, onion, mozzarella cheese, Gouda cheese, and cilantro.

5. Bake pizza in preheated oven for 12 to 15 minutes or until crust is golden brown.

Per serving 285 cal., 7 g total fat (1 g sat. fat), 30 mg chol., 562 mg sodium, 39 g carbo., 1 g fiber, 17 g pro.
Daily Values 4% vit. A, 4% vit. C, 9% calcium, 11% iron

Canadian Bacon, Sweet Onion, and Apple Pizza

Prep 20 minutes **Bake** 12 minutes
Makes 4 servings

Though bacon is not exactly a health food, It is a powerhouse of flavor, so you can use it sparingly. Lighten up with low-fat cheese, pile on the apples and onions, add a leafy green salad, and this pizza becomes a nutritious meal.

SUPER FOODS
Apple
Onion

	Olive oil cooking spray, *Mazola® Pure*
1	package (6.5-ounce) pizza crust mix, *Betty Crocker®*
$\frac{1}{3}$	cup hot water
$\frac{1}{4}$	cup unsweetened organic applesauce
$\frac{1}{4}$	cup light blue cheese salad dressing, *Bernstein's®*
$\frac{1}{2}$	cup shredded fat-free mozzarella cheese, *Lifetime®*
$\frac{1}{2}$	cup shredded low-fat mozzarella cheese, *Precious®*
$\frac{1}{2}$	cup chopped Golden Delicious apple
$\frac{1}{4}$	cup chopped sweet onion
$\frac{1}{2}$	cup chopped Canadian bacon, *John's®*
	Grated Parmesan cheese, *DiGiorno®* (optional)

1. Preheat oven to 450 degrees F. Coat a baking sheet with cooking spray; set aside.

2. In a medium bowl, combine pizza crust mix, hot water, and applesauce. Stir together until well moistened. Beat 20 times to form dough. Cover and let rest for 5 to 10 minutes.

3. Using floured fingers, press dough into a 12-inch circle on prepared baking sheet. Top with salad dressing, mozzarella cheeses, apple, onion, and Canadian bacon.

4. Bake pizza in preheated oven for 12 to 17 minutes or until crust is golden brown. Serve with grated Parmesan cheese (optional).

Per serving 272 cal., 7 g total fat (3 g sat. fat), 20 mg chol., 920 mg sodium, 39 g carbo., 2 g fiber, 18 g pro.
Daily Values 2% vit. A, 3% vit. C, 22% calcium, 13% iron

Portobello Pizza

Prep 35 minutes **Bake** 15 minutes
Makes 4 servings

SUPER FOODS
Mushrooms
Tomatoes
Onion

Olive oil cooking spray, *Mazola® Pure*
2   portobello mushrooms, stems removed
4   teaspoons light roasted garlic balsamic salad
     dressing, *Bernstein's®*
1   package (6.5-ounce) pizza crust mix, *Betty Crocker®*
½ teaspoon ground black pepper, *McCormick®*
½ teaspoon dried Italian seasoning, *McCormick®*
½ cup hot water
¾ cup organic chunky tomato sauce, *Muir Glen®*
½ cup shredded fat-free mozzarella cheese, *Lifetime®*
1   to 2 roma tomatoes, finely chopped
¼ cup shredded fresh basil
1   tablespoon finely chopped scallion (green onion)

1. Preheat oven to 450 degrees F. Coat 2 baking sheets with cooking spray; set aside.

2. Place mushrooms upside down on one of the prepared baking sheets. Pour 1 teaspoon of the salad dressing on each mushroom. Bake in preheated oven for 15 to 18 minutes. Place baking sheet on wire rack; set aside.

3. Meanwhile, in a medium bowl, combine pizza crust mix, pepper, and Italian seasoning. Stir in hot water until mixture is well moistened. Beat 20 times to form dough. Cover and let rest for 5 to 10 minutes.

4. In a small bowl, combine tomato sauce and the remaining 2 teaspoons salad dressing; set aside. Chop roasted mushrooms into bite-size pieces; set aside.

5. Using floured fingers, press dough into a 12-inch circle on the second prepared baking sheet.

6. Spread tomato sauce mixture evenly over dough, leaving a 1-inch border. Top with mozzarella cheese, chopped mushrooms, tomato, 1 tablespoon of the basil, and scallion.

7. Bake pizza in preheated oven for 15 to 18 minutes or until crust is golden brown. Sprinkle with remaining basil.

Per serving 219 cal., 4 g total fat (0 g sat. fat), 3 mg chol., 837 mg sodium, 39 g carbo., 3 g fiber, 13 g pro.
Daily Values 5% vit. A, 17% vit. C, 12% calcium, 15% iron

Creole Shrimp Pizza

Prep 20 minutes **Bake** 12 minutes
Makes 6 servings

1	cup fresh or frozen medium shrimp
	Olive oil cooking spray, *Mazola® Pure*
1	package (6.5-ounce) pizza crust mix, *Betty Crocker®*
1½	teaspoons Cajun seasoning, *McCormick®*
½	cup hot water
1	cup organic chunky tomato sauce, *Muir Glen®*
1	teaspoon crushed garlic, *Christopher Ranch®*
½	teaspoon hot pepper sauce, *Tabasco®*
1	cup low-fat shredded mozzarella, *Precious®*
½	cup frozen chopped onions, thawed, *Ore-Ida®*
⅓	cup frozen chopped green bell peppers, thawed, *Pictsweet®*

SUPER FOODS
Tomatoes
Garlic
Onions
Peppers

1. Thaw shrimp, if frozen. Preheat oven to 450 degrees F. Peel and devein shrimp. Rinse under cold water and pat dry with paper towels. Set aside. Coat a baking sheet with cooking spray; set aside.

2. In a medium bowl, combine pizza crust mix and Cajun seasoning. Stir in hot water until mixture is well moistened. Beat 20 times to form dough. Cover and let rest for 5 to 10 minutes.

3. Meanwhile, for sauce, in a small bowl, combine tomato sauce, garlic, and hot pepper sauce; set aside.

4. Using floured fingers, press dough into a 12-inch square on prepared baking sheet. Spread sauce evenly over dough, leaving a 1-inch border. Top with mozzarella cheese, onions, and peppers. Add shrimp.

5. Bake pizza in preheated oven 12 to 17 minutes or until crust is golden brown.

Per serving 230 cal., 6 g total fat (3 g sat. fat), 57 mg chol., 697 mg sodium, 26 g carbo., 2 g fiber, 17 g pro.
Daily Values 4% vit. A, 27% vit. C, 17% calcium, 13% iron

Garden Vegetable Calzone

Prep 25 minutes **Bake** 15 minutes
Makes 4 servings

SUPER FOODS

Oats
Broccoli
Tomatoes
Mushrooms
Onions

Olive oil cooking spray, *Mazola® Pure*

1	package (6.5-ounce) pizza crust mix, ***Betty Crocker®***
$\frac{1}{3}$	cup quick-cooking oats, ***Quaker®***
$\frac{1}{2}$	cup hot water
1	cup frozen chopped broccoli, ***Birds Eye®***
$\frac{1}{2}$	cup organic chunky tomato sauce, ***Muir Glen®***
$\frac{1}{4}$	cup sliced bottled mushrooms, ***Green Giant®***
$\frac{1}{4}$	cup frozen chopped onions, ***Ore-Ida®***
4	cloves roasted garlic, finely chopped, ***Christopher Ranch®***
3	tablespoons light cheese spread with garlic herbs, ***Rondele®***
3	tablespoons low-fat ricotta cheese, ***Precious®***

1. Preheat oven to 450 degrees F. Lightly coat a baking sheet with cooking spray; set aside.

2. In a medium bowl, combine pizza crust mix and oats. Stir in hot water until mixture is well moistened. Beat 20 times to form dough. Cover and let rest for 5 to 10 minutes.

3. Meanwhile, place broccoli in a large microwave-safe bowl. Cover and microwave on high setting (100% power) for 8 minutes. Stir in tomato sauce, mushrooms, onions, and garlic; set aside.

4. Using floured fingers, press dough into a 12-inch circle on prepared baking sheet. Spread half of dough with cheese spread, leaving a $\frac{1}{2}$-inch border. Spoon vegetable mixture over cheese spread and dot with ricotta cheese. Fold dough over filling and pinch edges together to seal.

5. Bake calzone in preheated oven for 15 to 20 minutes or until crust is golden brown.

Per serving 264 cal., 6 g total fat (2 g sat. fat), 16 mg chol., 669 mg sodium, 42 g carbo., 4 g fiber, 12 g pro.
Daily Values 11% vit. A, 46% vit. C, 9% calcium, 16% iron

Vegetarian

My Grandma Lorraine was a vegetarian. While other mothers were cooking pot roast, she roasted a medley of vegetables and tossed them with yogurt, dill, and whatever else she thought might spark the flavor. While I didn't follow in her vegetarian footsteps, I did inherit her love of experimenting with different tastes. This chapter is filled with popular entrées flavored with an evocative blend of herbs and spices instead of meat. Some, like Gumbo Ya-Ya, are meatless versions of classic favorites; others, like Whole Grain Portobello Bake, acquire a unique meaty goodness from grains and vegetables. If you crave carbs, try Black Bean-and-Sweet Potato Enchiladas for plenty of plant protein. Eating vegetarian—all the time or some of the time—adds essential vitamins and fiber to your diet and very well may lower your cholesterol and your food bills. Now that's something everybody can love.

The Recipes

Korean-Style Rice Bowl

Start to Finish 20 minutes
Makes 6 servings

2   packages (8.8 ounces each) cooked brown rice, *Uncle Ben's*®
    Ready Rice
1   bag (16-ounce) frozen Asian vegetable mix, *Birds Eye*®
1   cup frozen sweet soy beans (edamame)
1   tablespoon water
1   tablespoon toasted sesame oil, *Dynasty*®
1   bag (8-ounce) vegetable steak slices (soy protein),
    Morningstar Farms®
4   teaspoons red chili sauce, *A Taste of Thai*®
2   teaspoons toasted sesame seeds (optional)

SUPER FOODS
Whole grains
Soy

1. Prepare brown rice in the microwave according to package directions; set aside.

2. In a microwave-safe bowl, combine Asian vegetable mix, soy beans, and water. Cover and microwave on high setting (100% power) for 5 to 6 minutes. Drain and stir in sesame oil; set aside.

3. Place steak slices on a microwave-safe plate. Cover with plastic wrap and microwave on high setting (100% power) for 1 to 2 minutes. Toss with red chili sauce; set aside.

4. To serve, divide half of the rice among 4 serving bowls and top with vegetables. Place steak slices over vegetables. Top with remaining rice. Garnish with sesame seeds (optional).

Per serving 327 cal., 12 g total fat (2 g sat. fat), 3 mg chol., 657 mg sodium, 41 g carbo., 6 g fiber, 16 g pro.
Daily Values 24% vit. A, 41% vit. C, 11% calcium, 17% iron

Black Bean-and-
Sweet Potato
Enchiladas

Prep 25 minutes **Bake** 40 minutes
Makes 8 enchiladas

SUPER FOODS
Tomatoes
Beans
Chile peppers
Sweet potato
Onion

3	cups water
1	can (6-ounce) tomato paste, *Contadina®*
1	packet (1.62-ounce) enchilada sauce mix, *Lawry's®*
1	teaspoon ground cumin, *McCormick®*
1	teaspoon pumpkin pie spice, *McCormick®*
1	can (15-ounce) no-salt-organic added black beans, rinsed and drained, *Eden®*
1	can (14.5-ounce) diced organic tomatoes with basil and oregano, drained, *Muir Glen®*
1	can (4-ounce) diced green chiles, drained, *Ortega®*
8	8-inch whole wheat tortillas, *Mission®*
2	cans (15 ounces each) cut sweet potatoes, drained and chopped, *Princella®*
1	cup chopped red onion
	Reduced-fat shredded Mexican cheese blend, *Sargento®* (optional)

1. Preheat oven to 350 degrees F. In a medium saucepan, stir together water, tomato paste, enchilada sauce mix, cumin, and pumpkin pie spice. Bring to a boil over high heat. Remove from heat; cool. Divide ½ cup of the enchilada sauce mixture evenly among 4 au gratin dishes or spread in a 13×9-inch baking pan; set aside. Pour 1½ cups of the enchilada sauce mixture into a pie plate; set aside. In a medium bowl, combine black beans, tomatoes, and green chiles.

2. To assemble each enchilada, dip a tortilla into enchilada sauce mixture in pie plate; place on a cutting board. Place ⅓ cup of the black bean mixture, 2 tablespoons of the sweet potatoes, and 2 tablespoons of the onion across the center of the tortilla. Roll tightly and place, seam side up, in an au gratin dish or the baking pan. Repeat to make 8 enchiladas. (Place 2 enchiladas in each au gratin dish.) Cover loosely with aluminum foil.

3. Bake enchiladas in preheated oven for 40 to 45 minutes or until heated through. Top with cheese during the last 10 minutes of baking (optional).

4. Meanwhile, place remaining 1½ cups of the enchilada sauce mixture in a microwave-safe bowl. Cover and microwave on high setting (100% power) for 2 minutes or until hot. Serve with enchiladas.

Per enchilada 349 cal., 3 g total fat (1 g sat. fat), 0 mg chol., 1,094 mg sodium, 70 g carbo., 8 g fiber, 12 g pro.
Daily Values 176% vit. A, 69% vit. C, 13% calcium, 23% iron

Spicy Potato Tacos

Prep 15 minutes **Bake** 15 minutes
Makes 6 servings

1	tablespoon salt-free fajita seasoning, *Spice Hunter*®
1	tablespoon canola oil, *Wesson*®
1	bag (16-ounce) precooked diced red-skin potatoes, *Reser's*®
$\frac{1}{3}$	cup reduced-fat Mexican cheese blend, *Sargento*®
1	can (16-ounce) vegetarian refried beans, *Rosarita*®
$\frac{3}{4}$	cup cilantro-flavored salsa, *Pace*®
1	box (5.8-ounce) white corn taco shells, *Ortega*®
	Tomatoes, chopped (optional)
	Onions, chopped (optional)
	Packaged chopped romaine lettuce, *Fresh Express*® (optional)
	Radishes, sliced (optional)
	Cilantro-flavored salsa, *Pace*® (optional)

SUPER FOODS
Beans
Tomatoes

1. Preheat oven to 350 degrees F. Line a baking sheet with aluminum foil; set aside.

2. In a large bowl, stir together fajita seasoning and oil. Add potatoes and toss until well coated. Spread in a single layer on prepared baking sheet. Sprinkle with cheese. Bake in preheated oven for 15 minutes.

3. Meanwhile, in a microwave-safe bowl, stir together beans and the ¾ cup salsa. Cover and microwave on high setting (100% power) for 3 minutes.

4. Heat taco shells in oven for 3 to 5 minutes. Spoon bean mixture into heated taco shells. Top with potato mixture. Top with tomatoes and onions (optional). Serve with lettuce, radishes, and additional salsa (optional).

Per serving 306 cal., 11 g total fat (3 g sat. fat), 3 mg chol., 732 mg sodium, 59 g carbo., 6 g fiber, 9 g pro.
Daily Values 1% vit. A, 14% vit. C, 8% calcium, 3% iron

Gumbo Ya-Ya

Prep 10 minutes **Cook** 30 minutes
Makes 8 servings

SUPER FOODS
Tomatoes
Soy
Onions
Peppers

4	cups water
1	bag (16-ounce) frozen okra and tomatoes, *Pictsweet*®
1	bag (16-ounce) frozen veggie crumbles (soy protein), *Morningstar Farms*®
2	ribs celery, chopped
1	cup frozen chopped onions, *Ore-Ida*®
1	cup frozen crowder peas, *Pictsweet*®
½	cup frozen chopped green bell peppers, *Pictsweet*®
2	teaspoons salt-free herb seasoning blend, *Spice Hunter*®
1	teaspoon black and red pepper blend, *McCormick*®
1	can (15-ounce) organic Cajun beans and rice, *Eden*®

1. In a small stockpot, combine water, okra and tomatoes, veggie crumbles, celery, onions, crowder peas, bell peppers, herb seasoning blend, and pepper blend. Bring to a boil over high heat; reduce heat. Cover and simmer for 20 to 25 minutes or until vegetables are tender. Stir in beans and rice; simmer for 10 to 15 minutes more.

Per serving 265 cal., 5 g total fat (0 g sat. fat), 10 mg chol., 536 mg sodium, 36 g carbo., 7 g fiber, 20 g pro.
Daily Values 5% vit. A, 22% vit. C, 9% calcium, 20% iron

Mediterranean Chili

Prep 15 minutes **Cook** 30 minutes
Makes 6 servings

SUPER FOODS
Onions
Soy
Beans
Tomatoes

1	tablespoon canola oil, *Wesson*®
2	small zucchini, finely chopped
2	small yellow summer squash, finely chopped
1	cup frozen chopped onions, *Ore-Ida*®
1	package (12-ounce) frozen veggie crumbles (soy protein), *Morningstar Farms*®
1	packet (1.25-ounce) low-sodium taco seasoning mix, *McCormick*®
2	cans (15 ounces each) no-salt-added organic kidney beans, rinsed and drained, *Eden*®
1	can (14.5-ounce) diced tomatoes with basil and garlic, *Muir Glen*®
2	cups fat-free vegetable broth, *Health Valley*®
¼	cup red wine vinegar
1	teaspoon hot pepper sauce, *Tabasco*®

1. In a medium pot, heat oil over medium-high heat. Add zucchini, yellow summer squash, and onions. Cook and stir until tender. Stir in veggie crumbles and taco seasoning mix. Stir in beans, tomatoes, vegetable broth, vinegar, and hot pepper sauce. Bring to a boil; reduce heat. Simmer for 30 minutes. Serve with Parmesan cheese (optional).

Per serving 315 cal., 7 g total fat (1 g sat. fat), 14 mg chol., 1,200 mg sodium, 38 g carbo., 14 g fiber, 26 g pro.
Daily Values 15% vit. A, 30% vit. C, 12% calcium, 26% iron

Black Bean Stew with Sherried Corn

Start to Finish 30 minutes
Makes 6 servings

SUPER FOODS
Beans
Mango
Onions
Whole grains

FOR BLACK BEAN STEW:

- 3 cans (15 ounces each) no-salt-added organic black beans, rinsed and drained, *Eden*®
- 1 jar (16-ounce) peach-mango salsa, *Desert Pepper*®
- $\frac{1}{2}$ cup frozen chopped onions, *Ore-Ida*®
- $\frac{1}{4}$ cup light balsamic vinaigrette salad dressing, *Newman's Own*®
- 1 package (8.8-ounce) cooked brown rice, *Uncle Ben's*® *Ready Rice*
- $\frac{1}{4}$ cup chopped fresh cilantro

FOR SHERRIED CORN:

- 1 $\frac{1}{2}$ cups frozen organic whole-kernel corn, *Cascadian Farm*®
- $\frac{1}{2}$ cup frozen chopped onions, *Ore-Ida*®
- $\frac{1}{4}$ cup dry sherry, *Christian Brothers*®
- $\frac{1}{4}$ teaspoon salt
- $\frac{1}{3}$ cup light sour cream, *Horizon Organic*®
- Fresh cilantro, chopped (optional)

1. For Black Bean Stew, in a large pot, combine beans, salsa, onions, and salad dressing. Bring to a boil over high heat; reduce heat. Simmer for 15 minutes.

2. Place half of the bean mixture in a blender. Cover and place a clean towel on top of blender. Blend until mixture is almost smooth; stir back into mixture in pot. Stir in rice and the $\frac{1}{4}$ cup cilantro. Cover and keep warm over low heat until ready to serve, stirring occasionally.

3. For Sherried Corn, in a small pot, combine corn, onions, sherry, and salt. Bring to a boil over high heat; reduce heat. Simmer until liquid is reduced by half. Remove from heat and stir in sour cream.

4. To serve, ladle Black Bean Stew into 6 serving bowls. Top with Sherried Corn. Sprinkle with additional chopped cilantro (optional).

Per serving 364 cal., 5 g total fat (1 g sat. fat), 18 mg chol., 375 mg sodium, 60 g carbo., 12 g fiber, 19 g pro.
Daily Values 42% vit. A, 42% vit. C, 12% calcium, 21% iron

Moroccan Stew

Prep 10 minutes **Cook** 30 minutes
Stand 5 minutes **Makes** 4 servings

SUPER FOODS
Broccoli
Carrots
Beans
Tomatoes
Apricots
Onions
Citrus
Garlic
Cinnamon

1	container (32-ounce) vegetable broth, *Health Valley*®
1	box (5.7-ounce) curry-flavored couscous, *Near East*®
1	bag (12-ounce) frozen broccoli, cauliflower, and carrots, *Birds Eye*®
1	can (15-ounce) organic garbanzo beans, rinsed and drained, *Eden*®
1	can (14.5-ounce) organic diced tomatoes, *Muir Glen*®
1	cup dried apricots, *Sun-Maid*®
½	cup frozen chopped onions, *Ore-Ida*®
1	tablespoon lemon juice, *ReaLemon*®
2	teaspoons crushed garlic, *Christopher Ranch*®
1	teaspoon ground cinnamon, *McCormick*®
¼	teaspoon cayenne pepper, *McCormick*®

1. In a large pot, combine vegetable broth, curry packet from couscous, frozen vegetables, beans, tomatoes, apricots, onions, lemon juice, garlic, cinnamon, and cayenne pepper. Bring to a boil over medium-high heat; reduce heat. Simmer for 30 minutes. Stir in couscous and remove from heat. Cover and let stand for 5 minutes.

Per serving 407 cal., 3 g total fat (0 g sat. fat), 10 mg chol., 983 mg sodium, 81 g carbo., 12 g fiber, 18 g pro.
Daily Values 69% vit. A, 58% vit. C, 16% calcium, 22% iron

Whole Grain Portobello Bake

Prep 15 minutes **Bake** 1 hour 45 minutes
Makes 6 servings

Olive oil cooking spray, *Mazola® Pure*
1 package (6-ounce) portobello mushrooms, sliced
1 can (15-ounce) no-salt-added organic navy beans, rinsed and drained, *Eden®*
1 can (15-ounce) artichoke hearts in water, drained and quartered, *Maria®*
1 can (14.5-ounce) fire-roasted diced tomatoes, *Muir Glen®*
1 cup frozen chopped onions, *Ore-Ida®*
1 cup whole grain rice blend, *Rice Selects®*
2 teaspoons dried Italian seasoning, *McCormick®*
1 teaspoon crushed garlic, *Christopher Ranch®*
2 cups vegetable broth, *Health Valley®*

SUPER FOODS
Mushrooms
Beans
Tomatoes
Onions
Whole grains
Garlic

1. Preheat oven to 375 degrees F. Lightly coat a 2½-quart casserole with cooking spray; set aside.

2. In a large bowl, combine mushrooms, beans, artichoke hearts, tomatoes, onions, rice blend, Italian seasoning, and garlic. Transfer to prepared casserole. Pour in vegetable broth. Cover with aluminum foil.

3. Bake casserole in preheated oven for 1 hour and 45 minutes or until liquid is absorbed.

Per serving 239 cal., 3 g total fat (0 g sat. fat), 14 mg chol., 525 mg sodium, 41 g carbo., 9 g fiber, 15 g pro.
Daily Values 7% vit. A, 16% vit. C, 6% calcium, 20% iron

Fish & Seafood

Leaner than meat or chicken, fish is high in protein, low in calories, and terrific on taste. Growing up in the Pacific Northwest, I always had fish part of my diet, but it was in Wisconsin that I learned its true versatility. While I was a waitress in college, the restaurant where I worked grilled fish deckside in the summer and served it in ways I'd never heard of: flaky fish burgers on a buttery bun, shrimp tacos with fruity-hot salsa, fresh-from-the-lake flounder swimming in citrus sauce. These recipes will have you equally hooked. White fish is lowest in fat, so Halibut-and-Spinach Packets makes a health-conscious choice. Orange-Glazed Salmon is fattier but offers the benefits of vitamin C with cholesterol-reducing omega-3s. Miso-Glazed Tuna and Oven-Baked Catfish with Creole Tartar make inexpensive fish taste rich. Seafood is nature's best catch, so eat it often—grilled, steamed, or sauteed.

The Recipes

Herb-Crusted Salmon with Corn

Prep 15 minutes **Bake** 22 minutes
Makes 4 servings

1	pound fresh or frozen salmon fillets
	Olive oil cooking spray, *Mazola® Pure*
1½	cups frozen organic whole-kernel corn, thawed, *Cascadian Farm®*
1	jar (4.5-ounce) sliced mushrooms, drained, *Green Giant®*
3	tablespoons herbes de Provence, *McCormick®*
2	tablespoons chopped pimientos, *Dromedary®*
1	tablespoon chopped fresh flat-leaf parsley
1	tablespoon balsamic vinegar, *Alessi®*
½	teaspoon crushed garlic, *Christopher Ranch®*
2	teaspoons extra-virgin olive oil, *Bertolli®*
	Fresh flat-leaf parsley sprigs (optional)

SUPER FOODS
Salmon
Mushrooms
Garlic
Olive oil

1. Thaw fish, if frozen. Preheat oven to 350 degrees F. Rinse fish under cold water and pat dry with paper towels. Cut into 4 serving-size portions. Lightly coat a baking sheet with cooking spray; set aside.

2. In a microwave-safe bowl, combine corn, mushrooms, 1 teaspoon of the herbes de Provence, pimientos, chopped parsley, vinegar, and garlic; set aside. Sprinkle remaining herbes de Provence on a plate.

3. Brush fish with olive oil. Coat fish with remaining herbs; place on prepared baking sheet. Bake in preheated oven for 22 to 26 minutes or until fish flakes easily when tested with a fork. Do not overcook.

4. Cover corn mixture; microwave on high setting (100% power) for 2 to 2½ minutes. Serve with fish. Garnish with parsley sprigs (optional).

Per serving 303 cal., 15 g total fat (3 g sat. fat), 66 mg chol., 207 mg sodium, 17 g carbo., 3 g fiber, 26 g pro.
Daily Values 13% vit. A, 24% vit. C, 7% calcium, 11% iron

Broiled Salmon with Creamy Horseradish

Prep 15 minutes **Broil** 8 minutes
Makes 4 servings

SUPER FOODS
Salmon
Olive oil

Cream sauces have been the downfall of many a diet, but fat-free sour cream and heart-healthy olive oil keep calories in line. A 1-pound fillet will feed four when the fish is as rich as salmon.

1	pound fresh or frozen salmon fillets
	Olive oil cooking spray, *Mazola® Pure*
½	cup fat-free sour cream, *Horizon Organic®*
2	tablespoons prepared horseradish, *Morehouse®*
1	teaspoon Worcestershire sauce, *Lea & Perrins®*
2	teaspoons extra-virgin olive oil, *Bertolli®*
1½	teaspoons salt-free lemon-pepper seasoning, *McCormick®*

1. Thaw fish, if frozen. Preheat broiler. Rinse fish under cold water and pat dry with paper towels. Cut into 4 serving-size portions. Lightly coat a baking sheet with cooking spray; set aside.

2. In a small bowl, stir together sour cream, horseradish, and Worcestershire sauce. Cover and refrigerate until ready to serve.

3. Brush fish with olive oil; sprinkle with lemon-pepper seasoning. Place on prepared baking sheet.

4. Broil fish 4 to 6 inches from heat for 4 to 6 minutes per side or until fish flakes easily when tested with a fork. Do not overcook. Serve with sour cream mixture.

Per serving 257 cal., 15 g total fat (3 g sat. fat), 69 mg chol., 151 mg sodium, 6 g carbo., 0 g fiber, 24 g pro.
Daily Values 3% vit. A, 9% vit. C, 6% calcium, 4% iron

Orange-Glazed Salmon

Prep 10 minutes **Marinate** 1 hour **Stand** 30 minutes
Broil 8 minutes **Makes** 6 servings

1½	**pounds fresh or frozen salmon fillets**
½	**cup orange juice,** *Minute Maid*®
⅓	**cup orange marmalade,** *Smucker's*®
1	**tablespoon Dijon mustard,** *Grey Poupon*®
2	**teaspoons salt-free citrus-herb seasoning,** *Spice Islands*®
1	**teaspoon bottled minced ginger,** *Christopher Ranch*®
	Wilted arugula (optional)
	Orange wedges (optional)

SUPER FOODS
Salmon
Citrus
Ginger

1. Thaw fish, if frozen. Rinse fish under cold water and pat dry with paper towels. Cut into 6 serving-size portions. Place fish in a large zip-top plastic bag; set aside.

2. For marinade, in a small bowl, stir together orange juice, marmalade, mustard, citrus-herb seasoning, and ginger. Pour into zip-top bag with fish. Squeeze air from bag and seal. Gently massage bag to combine ingredients. Chill in the refrigerator for 1 to 2 hours.

3. Remove fish from refrigerator 30 minutes before cooking. Preheat broiler. Line a baking sheet or broiler pan with aluminum foil.

4. Remove fish from zip-top bag; discard marinade. Place fish on prepared baking sheet. Broil fish 4 to 6 inches from heat for 4 to 6 minutes per side or until fish flakes easily when tested with a fork. Do not overcook.

5. Serve fish with wilted arugula and orange wedges (optional).

Per serving 262 cal., 12 g total fat (2 g sat. fat), 66 mg chol., 137 mg sodium, 14 g carbo., 0 g fiber, 23 g pro.
Daily Values 2% vit. A, 20% vit. C, 3% calcium, 3% iron

Miso-Glazed Tuna

Prep 10 minutes **Marinate** 1 hour **Stand** 30 minutes
Broil 8 minutes **Makes** 6 servings

SUPER FOODS
Tuna
Onions
Ginger

6	fresh or frozen tuna steaks (about 1$\frac{1}{2}$ pounds total)
1	cup sake or white wine
2	scallions (green onions), finely chopped
$\frac{1}{4}$	cup wasabi ginger salad dressing, *Girard's*®
2	tablespoons white or yellow miso paste
2	tablespoons honey, *SueBee*®
	Steamed shredded carrots (optional)

1. Thaw fish, if frozen. Rinse fish under cold water and pat dry with paper towels. Place fish in a large zip-top plastic bag; set aside.

2. For marinade, in small bowl, whisk together sake, scallions, salad dressing, miso paste, and honey. Pour into zip-top bag with fish. Squeeze air from bag and seal. Gently massage bag to combine ingredients. Chill in the refrigerator for 1 to 2 hours.

3. Remove fish from refrigerator 30 minutes before cooking. Preheat broiler. Line a baking sheet or broiler pan with aluminum foil.

4. Remove fish from zip-top bag; discard marinade. Place fish on prepared baking sheet. Broil fish 4 to 6 inches from heat for 4 to 6 minutes per side or until fish flakes easily when tested with a fork. Do not overcook. Serve fish with steamed shredded carrots (optional).

Per serving 219 cal., 2 g total fat (0 g sat. fat), 51 mg chol., 299 mg sodium, 12 g carbo., 0 g fiber, 28 g pro.
Daily Values 2% vit. A, 3% vit. C, 3% calcium, 6% iron

Snapper with Roasted Pepper Coulis

Prep 15 minutes **Broil** 8 minutes
Makes 4 servings

We all need to eat more fish. This dish makes it easy to up your intake of fish. A snappy sauce brings out even the mildest fish's flavor. Try a red pepper puree—or coulis—it adds color plus immunity-boosting vitamin A.

SUPER FOODS
Peppers
Garlic

1	pound fresh or frozen red snapper fillets
	Olive oil cooking spray, *Mazola® Pure*
1	jar (15-ounce) roasted bell peppers, chopped, *Mezzetta®*
¼	cup organic chicken broth, *Swanson®*
2	tablespoons balsamic vinegar
1	teaspoon chopped garlic, *Christopher Ranch®*
1	tablespoon salt-free all-purpose seasoning, *McCormick®*
1	teaspoon salt-free lemon-pepper seasoning, *McCormick®*

1. Thaw fish, if frozen. Rinse fish under cold water and pat dry with paper towels. Remove bones from fish and cut into 4 serving-size portions. Preheat broiler. Line a baking sheet or broiler pan with aluminum foil and coat with cooking spray; set aside.

2. For red pepper coulis, place bell peppers, chicken broth, vinegar, and garlic in a blender. Cover and blend about 1 minute or until smooth. Transfer to microwave-safe bowl. Cover and microwave on high setting (100% power) for 1½ minutes; set aside.

3. Place fish on prepared baking sheet and lightly coat fish with cooking spray. In a small bowl, combine all-purpose seasoning and lemon-pepper seasoning. Sprinkle evenly over fish.

4. Broil fish 4 to 6 inches from heat for 4 to 6 minutes per side or until fish flakes easily when tested with a fork. Do not overcook. Serve with red pepper coulis.

Per serving 147 cal., 2 g total fat (0 g sat. fat), 42 mg chol., 137 mg sodium, 8 g carbo., 2 g fiber, 24 g pro.
Daily Values 2% vit. A, 343% vit. C, 4% calcium, 7% iron

Citrus Snapper with Orange Relish

Prep 15 minutes Marinate 30 minutes
Stand 30 minutes Grill 8 minutes
Makes 4 servings

SUPER FOODS
Citrus
Peppers
Onion

1 pound fresh or frozen red snapper fillets
1 can (8.4-ounce) mandarin oranges in juice, *Dole*®
2 tablespoons frozen limeade concentrate, thawed, *Minute Maid*®
1 teaspoon salt-free citrus-herb seasoning, *Spice Islands*®
1 cup roasted bell peppers, chopped, *Mezzetta*®
1 tablespoon chopped fresh cilantro
1 teaspoon chopped scallion (green onion)
1 teaspoon lime juice, *ReaLime*®
   Salt and ground black pepper
   Scallions (green onions), slivered (optional)

1. Thaw fish, if frozen. Rinse fish under cold water and pat dry with paper towels. Remove bones and cut into 4 serving-size portions. Place fish in a large zip-top plastic bag. Drain oranges, reserving juice. Set oranges aside.

2. For marinade, in a small bowl, combine reserved juice, limeade concentrate, and citrus-herb seasoning. Pour into bag with fish. Squeeze air from bag and seal. Gently massage bag to combine ingredients. Chill in the refrigerator for 30 to 60 minutes.

3. Set up grill for direct cooking over medium-high heat. Remove fish from the refrigerator 30 minutes before grilling. Oil grate when ready to start cooking.

4. For relish, chop oranges. In a medium bowl combine chopped oranges, bell peppers, cilantro, chopped scallion, and lime juice. Season with salt and black pepper; set aside.

5. Remove fish from zip-top bag; discard marinade. Place fish on hot oiled grill. Cook for 4 to 6 minutes per side or until fish flakes easily when tested with a fork. Do not overcook. Serve with relish. Garnish with slivered scallions (optional).

Per serving 163 cal., 1 g total fat (0 g sat. fat), 41 mg chol., 78 mg sodium, 13 g carbo., 1 g fiber, 24 g pro.
Daily Values 14% vit. A, 210% vit. C, 4% calcium, 5% iron

Halibut-and-Spinach Packets

Prep 15 minutes **Bake** 16 minutes
Makes 4 servings

1	pound fresh or frozen halibut fillets
1	teaspoon garlic pepper, *McCormick®*
1	box (10-ounce) frozen organic cut spinach, thawed, *Cascadian Farm®*
¼	cup chunky salsa, *Newman's Own®*
4	slices organic lemon
8	slices jalapeño chile pepper (see note, page 62)

SUPER FOODS
Spinach
Tomatoes
Citrus
Chile peppers

1. Thaw fish, if frozen. Preheat oven to 400 degrees F. Rinse fish under cold water and pat dry with paper towels. Cut into 4 serving-size portions. Sprinkle with garlic pepper; set aside. Cut four 12×10-inch pieces of parchment paper or aluminum foil; set aside. Squeeze excess water from spinach.

2. Place one-fourth of the spinach on a sheet of parchment paper. Top with a piece of fish. Add 1 tablespoon of the salsa, a lemon slice, and two slices of chile pepper. Fold parchment over fish; seal packet with a double-fold on each edge. Repeat to make 4 packets. Place packets on a baking sheet.

3. Bake fish in preheated oven for 16 to 20 minutes or until fish flakes easily when tested with a fork. Do not overcook.

Per serving 148 cal., 3 g total fat (0 g sat. fat), 36 mg chol., 315 mg sodium, 4 g carbo., 2 g fiber, 25 g pro.
Daily Values 106% vit. A, 20% vit. C, 11% calcium, 7% iron

Grilled Halibut with Peach-Habañero Sauce

Prep 15 minutes Marinate 1 hour
Stand 30 minutes Grill 8 minutes
Makes 6 servings

SUPER FOODS
Citrus
Garlic
Tomatoes
Chile peppers

1½	pounds fresh or frozen halibut fillets
1	cup peach nectar, *Kern's*®
¼	cup finely chopped fresh cilantro
3	tablespoons frozen limeade concentrate, thawed, *Minute Maid*®
2	teaspoons crushed garlic, *Christopher Ranch*®
1	tablespoon seafood grill and broil seasoning, *Spice Hunter*®
1	cup frozen peach slices, thawed and chopped, *Dole*®
⅔	cup petite-cut tomatoes with sweet onion and garlic, *S&W*®
2	tablespoons chopped fresh cilantro
1	tablespoon lime juice, *ReaLime*®
1	habañero or jalapeño chile pepper, finely chopped (see note, page 62)
	Lime wedges (optional)

1. Thaw fish, if frozen. Rinse fish under cold water and pat dry with paper towels. Cut into 6 serving-size portions. Place in a large zip-top plastic bag; set aside.

2. For marinade, in a small bowl, combine peach nectar, the ¼ cup cilantro, limeade concentrate, garlic, and seafood seasoning. Pour into zip-top bag with fish. Squeeze air from bag and seal. Gently massage bag to combine ingredients. Chill in the refrigerator for 1 to 2 hours.

3. Meanwhile, for sauce, in a medium bowl, stir together peaches, tomatoes, the 2 tablespoons cilantro, lime juice, and chile pepper. Cover and refrigerate for at least 1 hour before serving.

4. Set up grill for direct cooking over medium-high heat. Remove fish from the refrigerator 30 minutes before grilling. Oil grate when ready to start cooking.

5. Remove fish from zip-top bag; discard marinade. Place fish on hot oiled grill. Cook for 4 to 6 minutes per side or until fish flakes easily when tested with a fork. Do not overcook. Serve fish with sauce and lime wedges (optional).

Per serving 172 cal., 3 g total fat (0 g sat. fat), 36 mg chol., 201 mg sodium, 11 g carbo., 1 g fiber, 25 g pro.
Daily Values 11% vit. A, 20% vit. C, 7% calcium, 9% iron

Lemon Swordfish Brochettes

Prep 20 minutes Marinate 1 hour
Stand 30 minutes Grill 12 minutes
Makes 6 servings

In French, *en brochette* means "on a skewer." Instead of lemon butter, lemonade and grilled lemon wedges flavor the swordfish for a lighter, cleaner taste that oozes vitamin C.

SUPER FOODS
Citrus
Garlic
Tomatoes

1 $\frac{1}{2}$ pounds fresh or frozen swordfish steaks at least 1 inch thick
1   bottle (8-ounce) clam juice, *Snow's*®
$\frac{1}{3}$ cup finely chopped fresh flat-leaf parsley
$\frac{1}{3}$ cup white wine vinegar
3   tablespoons frozen lemonade concentrate, thawed, *Minute Maid*®
2   teaspoons salt-free lemon-pepper seasoning, *McCormick*®
2   teaspoons crushed garlic, *Christopher Ranch*®
24 cherry tomatoes
3   organic lemons, each cut into 8 pieces

1. Thaw fish, if frozen. Soak twelve 10-inch wooden skewers in water for 30 minutes. Meanwhile, rinse fish under cold water; pat dry with paper towels. Remove skin from fish; cut fish into 1-inch cubes.

2. For marinade, in small bowl, stir together clam juice, parsley, vinegar, lemonade concentrate, lemon-pepper seasoning, and garlic; set aside.

3. Drain skewers. Alternately thread fish pieces and tomatoes on skewers, beginning and ending each skewer with a lemon piece. Place skewers in 2 large shallow baking dishes. Pour marinade over skewers, dividing equally between baking dishes. Cover and chill in the refrigerator for 1 to 2 hours.

4. Set up grill for direct cooking over medium-high heat. Remove skewers from the refrigerator 30 minutes before grilling. Oil grate when ready to start cooking.

5. Remove skewers from baking dishes; discard marinade. Place skewers on hot oiled grill. Cook for 3 to 4 minutes per side (12 to 16 minutes total) or until fish flakes easily when tested with a fork. Do not overcook.

Per serving 184 cal., 5 g total fat (1 g sat. fat), 44 mg chol., 161 mg sodium, 12 g carbo., 3 g fiber, 24 g pro.
Daily Values 17% vit. A, 74% vit. C, 5% calcium, 11% iron

Garlicky
Shrimp Tacos

Start to Finish 15 minutes
Makes 4 servings

SUPER FOODS
Tomatoes
Garlic
Citrus

$\frac{2}{3}$ cup chunky salsa, *Newman's Own*®
$\frac{1}{3}$ cup fat-free sour cream, *Horizon Organic*®
$\frac{1}{4}$ cup oil-packed sun-dried tomatoes
8 ounces cooked shrimp
1 tablespoon chopped garlic, *Christopher Ranch*®
$\frac{3}{4}$ teaspoon salt-free Mexican seasoning, *Spice Hunter*®
2 tablespoons lime juice, *ReaLime*®
8 6-inch yellow corn tortillas, *Mission*®
2 cups coleslaw mix, *Fresh Express*®
2 limes, cut into wedges

1. In a small bowl, combine salsa and sour cream; set aside. Drain tomatoes, reserving 2 teaspoons of the oil. Cut tomatoes into strips.

2. In a medium nonstick skillet, heat the 2 teaspoons reserved oil over medium-high heat. Add tomatoes, shrimp, garlic, and Mexican seasoning. Cook and stir for 4 to 6 minutes or until heated through. Remove from heat and stir in lime juice.

3. Place tortillas on a microwave-safe plate. Cover and microwave on high setting (100% power) for 2 minutes.

4. To serve, fill each of the tortillas with ¼ cup of the coleslaw mix, ¼ cup of the shrimp mixture, and 2 tablespoons of the salsa mixture. Serve with lime wedges.

Per 2-taco serving 289 cal., 6 g total fat (1 g sat. fat), 88 mg chol., 373 mg sodium, 44 g carbo., 4 g fiber, 17 g pro.
Daily Values 15% vit. A, 61% vit. C, 15% calcium, 25% iron

Oven-Baked Catfish with Creole Tartar

Prep 15 minutes **Marinate** 30 minutes
Bake 15 minutes **Makes** 4 servings

1	pound fresh or frozen catfish fillets
	Olive oil cooking spray, *Mazola® Pure*
1 ½	cups buttermilk
2	teaspoons Cajun seasoning, *McCormick®*
½	cup reduced-fat mayonnaise, *Hellmann's® or Best Foods®*
1	tablespoon sweet pickle relish, *Vlasic®*
1	teaspoon Cajun seasoning, *McCormick®*
1	teaspoon lemon juice, *ReaLemon®*
½	teaspoon hot pepper sauce, *Tabasco®*
1 ½	cups cornflake crumbs, *Kellogg's®*
	Scallions (green onions), chopped (optional)

SUPER FOODS
Citrus

1. Thaw fish, if frozen. Preheat oven to 350 degrees F. Rinse fish under cold water and pat dry with paper towels. Cut into 4 serving-size portions. Place fish in a large zip-top plastic bag; set aside. Lightly coat baking sheet with cooking spray; set aside.

2. For marinade, in a small bowl, stir together buttermilk and the 2 teaspoons Cajun seasoning. Pour into zip-top bag with fish. Squeeze air from bag and seal. Gently massage bag to combine ingredients. Chill in the refrigerator for 30 minutes.

3. For tartar sauce, in a small bowl, combine mayonnaise, pickle relish, the 1 teaspoon Cajun seasoning, lemon juice, and hot pepper sauce. Cover and chill until ready to use.

4. Spread cornflake crumbs in a pie plate or shallow bowl. Remove fish from zip-top bag, shaking off any excess marinade; discard marinade. Coat fish with corn crumbs. Place on prepared baking sheet; lightly coat fish with cooking spray.

5. Bake fish in preheated oven for 15 minutes or until fish flakes easily when tested with a fork. Do not overcook. Top tartar sauce with chopped scallions (optional). Serve tartar sauce with fish.

Per serving 420 cal., 19 g total fat (4 g sat. fat), 67 mg chol., 799 mg sodium, 36 g carbo., 0 g fiber, 24 g pro.
Daily Values 3% vit. A, 4% vit. C, 13% calcium, 36% iron

Poultry

Maybe it's all the talk about chicken soup for the soul or the smell of barbecued chicken hot off the grill—whatever it is, chicken is the dish that draws hungry diners to the table again and again. As a child, I got my first taste of "real" cooking from fried chicken. I salted the chicken, dredged it in flour, fried it up, and felt like a grown-up. I learned from the Food Network Kitchens® that the healthiest way to prepare poultry is to remove the skin, which is full of unhealthy saturated fat. Grill, roast, or bake skinless, boneless poultry with fruits and vegetables and you'll get great flavor without tons of added fat. White meat is healthier than dark—and extra juicy when grilled with citrus fruits. Chicken with Green Beans and Lemongrass Sauce and Grilled Chicken with Grapefruit Salsa are light, fragrant, and look pretty on a plate. Instead of the usual meat loaf, bake the lower-calorie Turkey Loaf with Sun-Dried Tomatoes. Pretzel-Crusted Chicken with Honey Mustard Sauce is both a cook's and a diner's dream: fancy enough for food-loving gourmets, yet simple enough for the most finicky eaters—kids.

The Recipes

Cilantro-Pesto Chicken

Prep 10 minutes **Broil** 12 minutes
Makes 4 servings

SUPER FOODS
Walnuts
Olive oil
Garlic
Citrus

1 ¼ cups chopped fresh cilantro (about 1 bunch)
¼ cup reduced-sodium chicken broth, *Swanson*®
2 tablespoons walnuts, toasted
2 teaspoons extra-virgin olive oil, *Bertolli*®
½ teaspoon crushed garlic, *Christopher Ranch*®
½ teaspoon lemon juice, *ReaLemon*®
4 6-ounce boneless, skinless chicken breast halves
2 tablespoons extra-virgin olive oil, *Bertolli*®
2 teaspoons salt-free lemon-pepper seasoning, *McCormick*®
Salt (optional)
Broiled or grilled sweet bell pepper strips and/or onion wedges (optional)

1. For pesto, in a blender, combine cilantro, chicken broth, walnuts, the 2 teaspoons olive oil, garlic, and lemon juice. Cover and pulse until well combined, scraping down sides of blender. Set aside.

2. Preheat broiler.* Brush both sides of chicken pieces with the 2 tablespoons olive oil and sprinkle with lemon-pepper seasoning and salt (optional).

3. Broil chicken 4 to 5 inches from heat for 6 to 8 minutes per side or until chicken is no longer pink (165 degrees F).

4. Top hot chicken pieces with pesto. Serve with bell peppers and/or onions (optional).

*NOTE: Chicken also may be grilled. Set up grill for direct cooking over medium-high heat. Oil grate when ready to start cooking. Place chicken on hot oiled grill. Cook for 6 to 8 minutes per side or until chicken is no longer pink (165 degrees F).

Per serving 307 cal., 14 g total fat (2 g sat. fat), 98 mg chol., 142 mg sodium, 2 g carbo., 1 g fiber, 41 g pro.
Daily Values 30% vit. A, 15% vit. C, 5% calcium, 10% iron

Lemon-Rosemary Chicken

Prep 10 minutes **Bake** 20 minutes
Makes 4 servings

4	6-ounce boneless, skinless chicken breast halves
2	teaspoons extra-virgin olive oil, *Bertolli*®
1	teaspoon salt-free lemon-pepper seasoning, *McCormick*®
1	teaspoon salt-free citrus-herb seasoning, *Spice Islands*®
	Salt (optional)
3	organic lemons, thinly sliced
	Fresh rosemary sprigs
1	cup organic chicken broth, *Swanson*®
¼	cup white wine
½	teaspoon crushed garlic, *Christopher Ranch*®

SUPER FOODS
Olive oil
Citrus
Garlic

1. Preheat oven to 375 degrees F. Brush both sides of chicken pieces with olive oil and sprinkle with lemon-pepper seasoning, citrus-herb seasoning, and salt (optional); set aside.

2. In a baking dish, arrange 2 to 3 slices of lemon and a sprig of rosemary for each chicken piece. Place chicken, smooth sides up, on lemon and rosemary. Top each chicken piece with another sprig of rosemary and 2 to 3 slices of lemon.

3. Bake chicken in preheated oven for 20 to 25 minutes or until chicken is no longer pink (165 degrees F). Remove chicken to platter and cover with aluminum foil to keep warm.

4. In a small saucepan, combine half of the rosemary from the baking dish and any browned bits from baking dish. Add chicken broth, wine, and garlic. Bring to a boil over medium-high heat; cook until mixture is reduced by half. Using a fine-mesh strainer, strain mixture. Discard solids. Serve mixture with chicken. Garnish with additional lemon slices and rosemary sprigs.

Per serving 242 cal., 5 g total fat (1 g sat. fat), 99 mg chol., 315 mg sodium, 7 g carbo., 3 g fiber, 40 g pro.
Daily Values 1% vit. A, 70% vit. C, 6% calcium, 9% iron

Grilled Chicken with Grapefruit Salsa

Prep 10 minutes **Marinate** 1 hour
Grill 12 minutes **Makes** 4 servings

SUPER FOODS
Citrus
Olive oil
Chile peppers
Onion

4	6-ounce boneless, skinless chicken breast halves
1	jar (24-ounce) refrigerated red grapefruit segments, *Del Monte*®
¼	cup extra-virgin olive oil, *Bertolli*®
¼	cup finely chopped fresh mint
3	tablespoons finely chopped fresh cilantro
2	tablespoons lime juice, *ReaLime*®
1	tablespoon salt-free chicken seasoning, *McCormick*®
1	jalapeño chile pepper, finely chopped (see note, page 62)
1	scallion (green onion), finely chopped
1	teaspoon salt-free lemon-pepper seasoning, *McCormick*®
	Arugula (optional)

1. Place chicken pieces in a large zip-top plastic bag. Drain grapefruit, reserving ½ cup juice. Set grapefruit aside.

2. In a small bowl, combine the reserved grapefruit juice, olive oil, 2 tablespoons of the mint, 2 tablespoons of the cilantro, lime juice, and chicken seasoning. Pour mixture into zip-top bag with chicken. Squeeze air from bag and seal. Gently massage bag to combine ingredients. Chill in the refrigerator for 1 to 2 hours.

3. Set up grill for direct cooking over medium-high heat.* Remove chicken from refrigerator 30 minutes before grilling. Oil grate when ready to start cooking. Remove chicken from zip-top bag; discard marinade. Place chicken on hot oiled grill. Cook for 6 to 8 minutes per side or until no longer pink (165 degrees F).

4. For salsa, in a medium bowl, combine grapefruit, the remaining 2 tablespoons mint, the remaining 1 tablespoon cilantro, chile pepper, scallion, and lemon-pepper seasoning. Serve chicken with salsa and arugula (optional).

*NOTE: Chicken also may be broiled. Preheat broiler. Broil chicken 4 to 5 inches from heat source for 6 to 8 minutes per side or until no longer pink (165 degrees F).

Per serving 314 cal., 7 g total fat (1 g sat. fat), 99 mg chol., 114 mg sodium, 19 g carbo., 1 g fiber, 41 g pro.
Daily Values 7% vit. A, 140% vit. C, 5% calcium, 13% iron

Pretzel-Crusted Chicken with Honey Mustard Sauce

Prep 10 minutes **Bake** 10 minutes
Makes 4 servings

4	cups unsalted tiny pretzels, crushed, *Laura Scudder's*®
4	6-ounce boneless, skinless chicken breast halves, cut into 1-inch-thick strips
$\frac{3}{4}$	cup honey Dijon mustard, *French's*®
3	tablespoons organic chicken broth, *Swanson*®
$1\frac{1}{2}$	teaspoons dried Italian seasoning, *McCormick*®

1. Preheat oven to 375 degrees F. Line a baking sheet with aluminum foil; set aside. Put crushed pretzels in a pie plate; set aside.

2. Brush both sides of chicken pieces with ¼ cup of the honey mustard. Press chicken into crushed pretzels to coat. Place on the prepared baking sheet.

3. Bake chicken in preheated oven for 10 minutes or until chicken is no longer pink.

4. Meanwhile, in a small microwave-safe bowl, combine the remaining ½ cup honey mustard, chicken broth, and Italian seasoning. Microwave on high setting (100% power) for 1 minute or until heated through. Serve with chicken.

Per serving 455 cal., 5 g total fat (1 g sat. fat), 99 mg chol., 572 mg sodium, 54 g carbo., 2 g fiber, 45 g pro.
Daily Values 1% vit. A, 5% calcium, 21% iron

Island Chicken

Prep 10 minutes **Grill** 12 minutes
Makes 4 servings

4	6-ounce boneless, skinless chicken breast halves
2	teaspoons extra-virgin olive oil, *Bertolli*®
2½	teaspoons salt-free Jamaican jerk seasoning, *Spice Hunter*®
	Salt (optional)
1	can (20-ounce) pineapple slices (juice pack) *Dole*®
1	tablespoon packed brown sugar, *C&H*®
	Hot cooked brown rice (optional)

1. Set up grill for direct cooking over medium-high heat.* Oil grate when ready to start cooking.

2. Brush both sides of chicken pieces with olive oil and sprinkle with 1½ teaspoons of the jerk seasoning and salt (optional); set aside.

3. Drain pineapple slices, reserving juice. Sprinkle both sides of pineapple slices with ¾ teaspoon of the jerk seasoning; set aside.

4. For sauce, in small saucepan, combine reserved pineapple juice, the remaining ¼ teaspoon jerk seasoning, and brown sugar. Bring to a boil over high heat; cook about 5 minutes or until mixture is reduced by half. Set aside.

5. Place chicken on hot oiled grill. Cook for 6 to 8 minutes per side or until no longer pink (165 degrees F). Remove to a platter and cover with aluminum foil to keep warm.

6. Place pineapple slices on grill and cook for 1 to 2 minutes per side or until grill marks appear and pineapple is heated through.

7. Serve chicken with pineapple slices and sauce. Serve with hot cooked rice (optional).

*NOTE: Chicken also may be broiled. Preheat broiler. Broil chicken 4 to 5 inches from heat for 6 to 8 minutes per side or until no longer pink (165 degrees F). Broil pineapple 1 to 2 minutes per side or until warm.

Per serving 312 cal., 5 g total fat (1 g sat. fat), 99 mg chol., 95 mg sodium, 26 g carbo., 2 g fiber, 40 g pro.
Daily Values 2% vit. A, 22% vit. C, 5% calcium, 9% iron

Italian Chicken with Artichokes

Start to Finish 30 minutes
Makes 4 servings

SUPER FOODS
Onion
Garlic
Tomatoes

1½ pounds boneless, skinless chicken breast halves, cut into 1-inch pieces
1 teaspoon salt-free chicken seasoning, *McCormick®*
1 teaspoon dried Italian seasoning, *McCormick®*
   Olive oil cooking spray, *Mazola® Pure*
1 onion, chopped
1 teaspoon crushed garlic, *Christopher Ranch®*
1 can (15-ounce) artichoke hearts in water, drained and quartered, *Maria®*
1 can (14.5-ounce) organic diced tomatoes with basil, *Muir Glen®*
¾ cup Chardonnay or other white wine
2 tablespoons organic tomato paste, *Muir Glen®*
15 fresh basil leaves, torn
   Hot cooked whole wheat linguine (optional)
   Fresh basil sprigs (optional)

1. Sprinkle chicken pieces with chicken seasoning and Italian seasoning; set aside.

2. Coat a large nonstick skillet with cooking spray and heat over medium-high heat. Add chicken, onion, and garlic. Cook and stir for 8 to 10 minutes or until chicken is no longer pink. Stir in artichoke hearts, tomatoes, wine, and tomato paste. Bring to a boil; reduce heat. Stir in torn basil; simmer for 10 minutes.

3. Serve chicken over hot cooked linguine (optional). Garnish with basil sprigs (optional).

Per serving 318 cal., 3 g total fat (1 g sat. fat), 99 mg chol., 962 mg sodium, 20 g carbo., 4 g fiber, 44 g pro.
Daily Values 22% vit. A, 23% vit. C, 14% calcium, 29% iron

Chicken with Green Beans and Lemongrass Sauce

Start to Finish 25 minutes
Makes 4 servings

1	cup organic chicken broth, *Swanson®*
4	6-inch pieces fresh lemongrass, chopped
1½	pounds boneless, skinless chicken breast halves, cut into 1-inch pieces
2	teaspoons salt-free Thai seasoning, *Spice Hunter®*
	Canola oil cooking spray, *Mazola® Pure*
1	package (8-ounce) presliced fresh mushrooms
1	onion, chopped
1	teaspoon minced garlic, *Christopher Ranch®*
1	package (16-ounce) frozen cut green beans, thawed, *Birds Eye®*
1	can (14-ounce) light coconut milk, *A Taste of Thai®*
1	tablespoon lime juice, *ReaLime®*

SUPER FOODS
Mushrooms
Onion
Garlic
Green beans
Citrus

1. In a small saucepan, combine chicken broth and lemongrass. Bring to a boil over high heat; cook until mixture is reduced by half. Using a fine-mesh strainer, strain to remove solids. Set broth mixture aside; discard solids. Sprinkle both sides of chicken pieces with Thai seasoning; set aside.

2. Coat a large nonstick skillet with cooking spray; heat over medium-high heat. Add chicken, mushrooms, onion, and garlic. Cook for 8 to 10 minutes or until chicken is no longer pink.

3. Add green beans, coconut milk, and broth mixture. Bring to a boil; reduce heat. Simmer about 7 to 10 minutes or just until beans are tender, stirring occasionally. Stir in lime juice.

Per serving 323 cal., 9 g total fat (4 g sat. fat), 99 mg chol., 366 mg sodium, 17 g carbo., 4 g fiber, 44 g pro.
Daily Values 12% vit. A, 28% vit. C, 8% calcium, 18% iron

Provençal Turkey Breast

Prep 10 minutes **Bake** 1 hour
Stand 5 minutes **Makes** 6 servings

SUPER FOODS
Garlic
Olive oil
Citrus

Low-fat protein foods such as turkey white meat are even better baked. To add a wonderfully earthy flavor, slit pockets and insert garlic cloves and rub with pungent herbes de Provence and Dijon mustard.

> **Olive oil cooking spray, *Mazola® Pure***
> 2 **pounds boneless, skinless turkey breast**
> 10 **roasted whole garlic cloves, *Christopher Ranch®***
> ¼ **cup Dijon mustard, *Grey Poupon®***
> 1 **tablespoon herbes de Provence, *McCormick®***
> 1 **tablespoon extra-virgin olive oil, *Bertolli®***
> 1 **organic lemon, thinly sliced**
> 18 **garlic-stuffed green olives, *Mezzetta®***
> **Fresh thyme sprigs (optional)**

1. Preheat oven to 350 degrees F. Lightly coat a 13×9-inch baking dish with cooking spray; set aside.

2. With a paring knife, cut 10 slits randomly into turkey breast and insert a roasted garlic clove into each slit; set aside. In a small bowl, stir together mustard, herbes de Provence, and oil; set aside.

3. Cover bottom of prepared baking dish with a layer of lemon slices. Arrange olives evenly over lemon slices. Top with turkey, making sure some olives are beneath turkey. Spread mustard mixture evenly over top of turkey.

4. Bake turkey in preheated oven for 60 to 70 minutes or until turkey is no longer pink (165 degrees F). Place baking dish on a wire rack. Cover with aluminum foil to keep warm. Let stand 5 to 10 minutes before slicing. Garnish with thyme (optional).

Per serving 221 cal., 4 g total fat (1 g sat. fat), 94 mg chol., 531 mg sodium, 6 g carbo., 1 g fiber, 40 g pro.
Daily Values 2% vit. A, 26% vit. C, 7% calcium, 14% iron

Turkey Loaf with Sun-Dried Tomatoes

Prep 20 minutes **Bake** 55 minutes
Makes 8 servings

	Olive oil cooking spray, *Mazola® Pure*
½	cup organic chicken broth, *Swanson®*
¼	cup frozen chopped onions, *Ore-Ida®*
¼	cup frozen chopped green bell peppers, *Pictsweet®*
¼	cup chopped celery
1	teaspoon crushed garlic, *Christopher Ranch®*
2	pounds ground uncooked turkey breast
1	cup cooked brown rice, *Uncle Ben's® Ready Rice*
¼	cup oil-pack sun-dried tomatoes, drained and finely chopped, *Alessi®*
1	egg
1	tablespoon Greek seasoning, *Spice Islands®*
¼	cup organic ketchup, *Hunt's®*

SUPER FOODS
Onions
Peppers
Garlic
Whole grains
Tomatoes
Egg

1. Preheat oven to 350 degrees F. Lightly coat a 9×5×3-inch loaf pan with cooking spray; set aside.

2. In a microwave-safe bowl, combine chicken broth, onions, peppers, celery, and garlic. Cover and microwave on high setting (100% power) for 5 minutes; cool.

3. In a large bowl, combine cooled vegetables, turkey, rice, tomatoes, egg, and Greek seasoning. With clean hands, thoroughly combine ingredients. Lightly pat mixture into prepared loaf pan. Spread ketchup on top.

4. Bake turkey loaf in preheated oven for 55 to 60 minutes or until no longer pink (165 degrees F).*

*NOTE: The internal color of a meat loaf is not a reliable doneness indicator. A turkey or chicken loaf cooked to 165 degrees F is safe, regardless of color. To measure the doneness of a meat loaf, insert an instant-read thermometer into the center of the loaf.

Per serving 180 cal., 3 g total fat (1 g sat. fat), 74 mg chol., 278 mg sodium, 8 g carbo., 1 g fiber, 29 g pro.
Daily Values 3% vit. A, 10% vit. C, 1% calcium, 10% iron

Spicy Turkey Meatballs in Tomato Sauce

Prep 20 minutes **Cook** 15 minutes
Makes 6 servings

2	slices whole grain bread, *Oroweat Health Nut*®
1⅓	cups organic chicken broth, *Swanson*®
1½	pounds ground uncooked turkey breast
1	cup frozen chopped onions, thawed, *Ore-Ida*®
1	tablespoon low-sodium chili seasoning, *McCormick*®
1	teaspoon ground cinnamon, *McCormick*®
1	teaspoon black and red pepper blend, *McCormick*®
1	jar (25.5-ounce) organic Italian herb pasta sauce, *Muir Glen*®
	Hot cooked brown rice (optional)
	Fresh flat-leaf parsley, chopped (optional)

1. Tear bread into pieces; place in a food processor or blender. Cover and process or blend until fine crumbs form. Transfer to a bowl and stir in ⅓ cup of the chicken broth; set aside.

2. In a large bowl, combine turkey, onions, chili seasoning, cinnamon, and pepper blend. Add soaked bread crumbs. With clean hands, thoroughly combine ingredients. Wet hands to keep mixture from sticking. Shape mixture into thirty-two 1-inch meatballs; set aside.

3. In a large skillet, combine pasta sauce and the remaining 1 cup of broth. Bring to a boil over medium-high heat, stirring occasionally.

4. Carefully add meatballs, one at a time. Return to a boil, using a large spoon to turn meatballs. Reduce heat to medium-low; simmer for 15 minutes.

5. Serve meatballs over hot cooked rice (optional). Garnish with parsley (optional).

Per serving 211 cal., 3 g total fat (1 g sat. fat), 46 mg chol., 685 mg sodium, 20 g carbo., 1 g fiber, 29 g pro.
Daily Values 23% vit. A, 17% vit. C, 6% calcium, 17% iron

Turkey-and-Red Bean Gumbo

Start to Finish 40 minutes
Makes 8 servings

	Olive oil cooking spray, *Mazola® Pure*
2	pounds boneless, skinless turkey breast, cut into bite-size pieces
6	cups organic low-sodium chicken broth, *Pacific Foods®*
1	can (15-ounce) no-salt-added organic kidney beans, rinsed and drained, *Eden®*
1	can (14.5-ounce) diced tomatoes with onion, celery, and bell pepper, *Hunt's®*
1	package (6.4-ounce) Cajun red beans and rice, *Knorr® or Lipton®*

SUPER FOODS
Beans
Tomatoes

1. Coat a large nonstick skillet with cooking spray; heat over medium-high heat. Add turkey pieces; cook and stir for 8 to 10 minutes or until no longer pink.*

2. Place turkey in a 4-quart pot. Stir in chicken broth, beans, tomatoes, and red beans and rice. Bring to a boil over high heat; reduce heat to low. Cover and simmer for 25 minutes.

*NOTE: Gumbo may also be cooked in a 4-quart slow cooker. Do not cook turkey in skillet. Combine all ingredients in a 4- to 5-quart slow cooker. Cover and cook on LOW heat setting for 6 to 8 hours.

Per serving 234 cal., 2 g total fat (1 g sat. fat), 70 mg chol., 269 mg sodium, 18 g carbo., 5 g fiber, 36 g pro.
Daily Values 2% vit. A, 3% vit. C, 6% calcium, 16% iron

King Ranch-Style Casserole

Prep 25 minutes **Bake** 25 minutes
Makes 8 servings

SUPER FOODS
Onions
Peppers
Garlic
Mushrooms
Yogurt
Tomatoes

	Olive oil cooking spray, *Mazola® Pure*
8	6-inch yellow corn tortillas, *Mission®*
1	cup organic chicken broth, *Swanson®* (optional)
1	cup frozen chopped onions, *Ore-Ida®*
1	cup frozen chopped green bell peppers, *Pictsweet®*
2	tablespoons organic chicken broth, *Swanson®*
1½	teaspoons crushed garlic, *Christopher Ranch®*
1	pound boneless, skinless turkey breast, cut into bite-size pieces
1	package (8-ounce) presliced fresh mushrooms
2	cups plain fat-free yogurt, *Horizon Organic®*
1	can (15-ounce) artichoke hearts in water, drained and chopped, *Maria®*
1	can (14.5-ounce) organic diced tomatoes, drained, *Muir Glen®*
3	tablespoons quick-mixing flour, *Wondra®*
2	tablespoons low-sodium chili seasoning, *McCormick®*
1½	cups organic shredded Jack cheese, *Horizon Organic®*
½	cup crushed baked tortilla chips, *Guiltless® Gourmet*

1. Preheat oven to 350 degrees F. Coat eight 10-ounce casseroles (or a 13×9-inch baking dish) with cooking spray; set aside. If desired, place tortillas in a pie plate with the 1 cup chicken broth to soften. (Complete this step if using the 13×9-inch baking dish; it is optional for 10-ounce casseroles.) Turn occasionally to ensure all tortillas are soaked.

2. In a microwave-safe bowl, combine onions, peppers, the 2 tablespoons chicken broth, and garlic. Cover and microwave on high setting (100% power) for 5 minutes; set aside.

3. Coat a large nonstick skillet with cooking spray. Heat over medium-high heat; add turkey pieces and mushrooms. Cook and stir for 7 to 9 minutes or until turkey is no longer pink. Stir in onion mixture, yogurt, artichokes, tomatoes, flour, and chili seasoning. Bring to a boil; reduce heat. Simmer for 5 minutes. Meanwhile, line each prepared casserole with a tortilla or place 4 tortillas in the bottom of the prepared baking dish, tearing to fit. Divide turkey mixture evenly among casseroles. Sprinkle with cheese and crushed tortilla chips. (For baking dish, layer half of turkey mixture and half of cheese into dish; repeat layers. Sprinkle with crushed tortilla chips.)

4. Bake in preheated oven for 25 minutes for individual casseroles (or 45 to 55 minutes for baking dish) or until mixture is golden and bubbly.

Per serving 322 cal., 9 g total fat (5 g sat. fat), 66 mg chol., 534 mg sodium, 28 g carbo., 4 g fiber, 30 g pro.
Daily Values 10% vit. A, 28% vit. C, 35% calcium, 18% iron

Meat

Prime rib. Bratwurst. Filet mignon. I ate them all—all the time! Then a good friend of mine had heart surgery, and I became much more vigilant about the meat in my diet. While meat has become mealtime's "bad boy," the truth is, we need meat in moderation. Rich in protein, B vitamins, and iron, meat forms the building blocks for muscles and bones, replacing cells and tissues the body needs. These recipes bring out meat's good side by using the leanest cuts—grilled, roasted, or baked—to reduce fat, not flavor. For even more health benefits, pair meat with super foods, such as fruit, vegetables, pasta, or grains. Stick to white meats with nutrient-rich sauces—Pork Medallions with Brandied Apples is a good example—and save red meat for special meals. Seared Beef Tenderloin with Blackberry-Merlot Sauce makes an impressive splurge for company—or for the family!

The Recipes

Blue Cheese-Crusted Filet Mignon

Start to Finish 20 minutes
Makes 4 servings

SUPER FOODS
Olive oil
Onions
Garlic

¼ cup plain bread crumbs, *Progresso*®
2 tablespoons blue cheese crumbles, *Treasure Cave*®
2 teaspoons fines herbes, *Spice Islands*®
½ teaspoon extra-virgin olive oil, *Bertolli*®
 Olive oil cooking spray, *Mazola*® *Pure*
4 4-ounce filet mignon steaks
½ teaspoon ground black pepper, *McCormick*®
½ cup cognac
1 cup organic beef broth, *Swanson*®
¼ cup frozen chopped onions, *Ore-Ida*®
1 teaspoon crushed garlic, *Christopher Ranch*®
 Salt and ground black pepper

1. Preheat oven to 400 degrees F. Line a baking sheet with aluminum foil; set aside.

2. In a small bowl, combine bread crumbs, blue cheese, fines herbes, and olive oil; set aside.

3. Coat a large skillet with cooking spray; heat over medium-high heat. Season steaks with the ½ teaspoon pepper and add to skillet. Cook for 2 minutes per side. Remove skillet from heat and transfer steaks to prepared baking sheet.

4. Top each steak with one-fourth of the blue cheese mixture. Roast in preheated oven for 4 minutes for medium-rare (145 degrees F) or 6 minutes for medium (160 degrees F).

5. For sauce, return skillet to heat and deglaze with cognac by scraping bits from bottom of skillet. Add beef broth, onions, and garlic. Bring to a boil over high heat; cook until mixture is reduced by half. Using a fine-mesh strainer, strain sauce. Discard solids. Season sauce with salt and additional pepper. Serve with steaks.

Per serving 306 cal., 11 g total fat (4 g sat. fat), 73 mg chol., 515 mg sodium, 7 g carbo., 1 g fiber, 26 g pro.
Daily Values 2% vit. A, 2% vit. C, 6% calcium, 20% iron

Seared Beef Tenderloin with Blackberry-Merlot Sauce

Start to Finish 20 minutes
Makes 4 servings

Olive oil cooking spray, *Mazola® Pure*
4 4-ounce beef tenderloin steaks
½ tablespoon salt-free all-purpose seasoning, *McCormick®*
½ cup Merlot or other red wine
½ cup blackberry preserves, *Dickinson's®*
½ teaspoon crushed garlic, *Christopher Ranch®*
Fresh blackberries (optional)
Fresh chives, sliced (optional)

SUPER FOODS
Blackberries
Garlic

1. Preheat oven to 400 degrees F. Line a baking sheet with aluminum foil; set aside.

2. Coat a large skillet with cooking spray; heat over medium-high heat. Sprinkle both sides of steaks with all-purpose seasoning. Place steaks in skillet. Cook for 2 minutes on each side. Remove skillet from heat and transfer steaks to prepared baking sheet.

3. Roast steaks in preheated oven for 4 minutes for medium rare (145 degrees F) or 6 minutes for medium (160 degrees F).

4. For sauce, return skillet to heat and deglaze with half of the wine by scraping bits from bottom of skillet. Return to medium-high heat and add remaining wine, blackberry preserves, and garlic. Bring to a boil; reduce heat. Simmer until mixture is reduced by half, stirring occasionally. Serve sauce with steaks. Garnish with blackberries and chives (optional).

Per serving 313 cal., 8 g total fat (3 g sat. fat), 70 mg chol., 66 mg sodium, 29 g carbo., 0 g fiber, 24 g pro.
Daily Values 6% vit. C, 2% calcium, 18% iron

Italian Beef

Prep 10 minutes **Marinate** 1 hour
Stand 30 minutes **Grill** 12 minutes **Makes** 6 servings

SUPER FOODS
Tomatoes
Garlic

Organic pasta sauce, garlic, and red wine turn ordinary flank steak into an extraordinary eating experience. Marinate extra-lean meat to tenderize it and lock in flavor. Magnifico!

1 ½	**pounds beef flank steak**
1 ½	**cups organic tomato basil pasta sauce,** *Muir Glen®*
½	**cup light Italian salad dressing,** *Newman's Own®*
1	**tablespoon chopped garlic,** *Christopher Ranch®*
¼	**cup red wine, Chianti**
1	**teaspoon dried Italian seasoning,** *McCormick®*
	Grilled green and/or red bell pepper wedges (optional)
	Grilled onion slices (optional)

1. Rinse steak under cold water and pat dry with paper towels. Place in a large zip-top plastic bag.

2. For marinade, in a bowl, combine ½ cup of the pasta sauce, salad dressing, and garlic. Add to zip-top bag with steak. Squeeze air from bag and seal. Gently massage bag to combine ingredients. Marinate in the refrigerator for 1 to 8 hours.

3. Set up grill for direct cooking over high heat. Remove steak from the refrigerator 30 minutes before cooking. Oil grate when ready to start cooking.

4. Remove steak from zip-top bag; discard marinade. Place steak on hot oiled grill. Cook for 6 to 7 minutes per side.

5. Meanwhile, for sauce, in a small saucepan, combine remaining pasta sauce, wine, and Italian seasoning. Bring to a boil over medium-high heat. Serve with steak. Serve steak with grilled peppers and onions (optional).

Per serving 227 cal., 9 g total fat (3 g sat. fat), 39 mg chol., 419 mg sodium, 7 g carbo., 1 g fiber, 26 g pro.
Daily Values 8% vit. A, 14% vit. C, 7% calcium, 14% iron

Adobo Beef

Prep 10 minutes **Marinate** 4 hours
Stand 30 minutes **Grill** 10 minutes **Makes** 4 servings

4	4-ounce beef tenderloin steaks
1	can (7-ounce) chipotle peppers in adobo sauce, *Embasa®*
1	cup organic beef broth *Swanson®*
¼	cup tequila, *José Cuervo®*
2	tablespoons frozen orange juice concentrate, thawed, *Minute Maid®*
1	tablespoon salt-free Mexican seasoning, *Spice Hunter®*
½	cup organic tomato sauce, *Muir Glen®*
½	teaspoon salt-free Mexican seasoning, *Spice Hunter®*
	Fresh cilantro leaves (optional)
	Black-eyed peas* (optional)

SUPER FOODS

Chile peppers
Citrus
Tomatoes

1. Rinse steaks under cold water and pat dry with paper towels. Place in a large zip-top plastic bag. Drain chipotle peppers, reserving 3 tablespoons of the adobo sauce. Chop enough pepper to make 1 tablespoon. Reserve remaining chipotle peppers and adobo sauce for another use.

2. For marinade, in a bowl, combine ¾ cup of the beef broth, tequila, orange juice concentrate, the 1 tablespoon Mexican seasoning, chopped chipotle pepper, and 2 tablespoons of the reserved adobo sauce. Add to zip-top bag with steaks. Squeeze air from bag and seal. Gently massage bag to combine ingredients. Marinate in the refrigerator for 4 to 8 hours.

3. Set up grill for direct cooking over high heat. Remove steaks from the refrigerator 30 minutes before cooking. Oil grate when ready to start cooking.

4. Remove steaks from zip-top bag; discard marinade. Place steaks on hot oiled grill. Cook for 5 to 6 minutes per side for medium (160 degrees F).

5. For sauce, in a microwave-safe bowl, combine tomato sauce, the ½ teaspoon Mexican seasoning, the remaining ¼ cup beef broth, and the remaining 1 tablespoon adobo sauce. Cover and microwave on high setting (100% power) for 1½ minutes. Spoon over steaks. Garnish with cilantro (optional). Serve with black-eyed peas (optional).

*NOTE: For an easy side dish, heat canned black-eyed peas with chopped celery and chopped carrot.

Per serving 245 cal., 9 g total fat (3 g sat. fat), 70 mg chol., 455 mg sodium, 7 g carbo., 1 g fiber, 25 g pro.
Daily Values 4% vit. A, 24% vit. C, 1% calcium, 19% iron

Grilled Jerk Pork

Prep 5 minutes **Marinate** 4 hours **Stand** 30 minutes + 5 minutes
Grill 20 minutes **Makes** 6 servings

SUPER FOODS
Mango
Garlic

1 ½   pounds pork tenderloin
1   bottle (12-ounce) fat-free mango salad dressing, *Consorzio*®
½   cup mango-flavored rum, *Malibu*®
2   tablespoons salt-free Jamaican jerk seasoning, *Spice Hunter*®
2   teaspoons crushed garlic, *Christopher Ranch*®
      Mango slices (optional)
      Fresh cilantro sprigs (optional)
      Lime wedges (optional)

1. Rinse tenderloin under cold water and pat dry with paper towels. Trim any fat or silver skin from pork. Place in a large zip-top plastic bag.

2. For marinade, in a bowl, combine salad dressing, rum, jerk seasoning, and garlic. Pour into zip-top bag with pork. Squeeze air from bag and seal. Gently massage bag to combine ingredients. Marinate in the refrigerator for 4 to 6 hours.

3. Set up grill for direct cooking over high heat. Remove pork from the refrigerator 30 minutes before cooking. Oil grate when ready to start cooking.

4. Remove pork from zip-top bag; discard marinade. Place pork on hot oiled grill. Cook for 20 to 28 minutes or until internal temperature reaches 160 degrees F, turning to cook all sides evenly.

5. Remove from grill; let stand for 5 minutes before slicing. Serve with mango slices, cilantro, and lime wedges (optional).

Per serving 185 cal., 3 g total fat (1 g sat. fat), 73 mg chol., 66 mg sodium, 8 g carbo., 0 g fiber, 24 g pro.
Daily Values 2% vit. C, 1% calcium, 8% iron

Herbed Pork with Honey Dijon Mustard

Prep 10 minutes **Roast** 18 minutes
Makes 4 servings

Olive oil cooking spray, *Mazola® Pure*
1   pound pork tenderloin
½   cup honey Dijon mustard, *French's®*
2   tablespoons fines herbes, *Spice Islands®*
1   cup frozen pearl onions, thawed, *C&W®*
½   cup organic chicken broth, *Swanson®*
1   teaspoon fines herbes, *Spice Islands®*
Fresh thyme sprigs (optional)

SUPER FOODS
Onions

1. Preheat oven to 400 degrees F. Line a baking sheet with aluminum foil; coat with cooking spray. Set aside.

2. Rinse tenderloin under cold water and pat dry with paper towels. Trim any fat and silver skin from pork. Cut into 4 portions. Brush ¼ cup of the honey mustard onto pork. Sprinkle with the 2 tablespoons fines herbes. Place on prepared baking sheet.

3. Roast in preheated oven for 18 to 25 minutes or until a meat thermometer registers 160 degrees F.

4. Meanwhile, in a small saucepan, combine onions and chicken broth. Cook over medium-high heat until onions are tender and liquid is reduced by half. Stir in the remaining ¼ cup honey mustard and the 1 teaspoon fines herbes. Serve with pork. Garnish with thyme (optional).

Per serving 227 cal., 3 g total fat (1 g sat. fat), 73 mg chol., 538 mg sodium, 23 g carbo., 1 g fiber, 28 g pro.
Daily Values 3% vit. A, 2% vit. C, 6% calcium, 14% iron

Roasted Basil-Pork Medallions with Red Grapes

Start to Finish 35 minutes
Makes 6 servings

Olive oil cooking spray, *Mazola® Pure*
2   pounds pork tenderloin
1   packet (0.88-ounce) garlic and basil vegetable seasoning, *McCormick®*
1½ cups seedless red grapes
½   cup sherry, *Christian Brothers®*
    Hot cooked couscous (optional)
    Sliced almonds, toasted, Planters® (optional)

1. Preheat oven to 400 degrees F. Lightly coat a shallow baking pan with cooking spray; set aside.

2. Rinse tenderloin under cold water and pat dry with paper towels. Trim any fat and silver skin from pork. Cut into 1-inch slices. Using a meat mallet or a small pot, pound pork pieces to a ¼-inch thickness.

3. Remove bag from seasoning packet. Place pork in bag with vegetable seasoning mix and shake until pieces are coated.

4. Arrange pork pieces in a single layer in prepared baking pan. Roast in preheated oven about 10 minutes or until cooked through. Transfer pieces to a platter; cover with aluminum foil to keep warm.

5. Put grapes in same baking pan and pour sherry over grapes. Roast about 10 minutes or until grape skins just begin to split. Return pork and juices to baking pan; spoon grapes over pork. Roast 5 minutes more.

6. To serve, divide couscous among 6 dinner plates (optional). Top with pork and grapes. Sprinkle with almonds (optional).

Per serving 247 cal., 5 g total fat (2 g sat. fat), 97 mg chol., 343 mg sodium, 11 g carbo., 0 g fiber, 32 g pro.
Daily Values 1% vit. A, 9% vit. C, 1% calcium, 12% iron

Jalapeño Pork Roll-Ups

Start to Finish 35 minutes
Makes 4 servings

Pork tenderloin is quite lean compared with other meats. This one is classically prepared with sweet applesauce and also includes a modern twist—jalapeño peppers, which help make it a mini fiesta. Roll the pork with jalapeño cream cheese spread and sauce it with a feisty jalapeño-tequila jelly.

1	pound pork loin
2	teaspoons salt-free fajita seasoning, *Spice Hunter®*
¼	cup light jalapeño cream cheese spread, *Kraft®*
	Olive oil cooking spray, *Mazola® Pure*
¼	cup jalapeño jelly, *Knott's Berry Farm®*
2	tablespoons tequila, *José Cuervo®*

1. Preheat oven to 400 degrees F. Line a baking sheet with aluminum foil; set aside. Slice pork into four portions ½ inch thick.

2. Using the smooth side of a meat mallet or a small pot, pound pork pieces to a ¼-inch thickness. Sprinkle both sides of pork pieces with fajita seasoning. Spread 1 tablespoon of cream cheese in center of each piece of pork; roll up. Secure with short wooden skewers.

3. Coat a large nonstick skillet with cooking spray; heat over medium-high heat. Place pork rolls, seam sides down, in skillet. Cook 1 minute per side (4 minutes total). Transfer to prepared baking sheet.

4. In a small saucepan, combine jalapeño jelly and tequila. Heat and stir until jelly has melted. Spoon over pork.

5. Roast in preheated oven for 15 to 20 minutes or until pork is cooked through.

Per serving 251 cal., 7 g total fat (3 g sat. fat), 78 mg chol., 173 mg sodium, 14 g carbo., 0 g fiber, 26 g pro.
Daily Values 2% vit. A, 2% vit. C, 7% calcium, 4% iron

Pork Marsala

Start to Finish 30 minutes
Makes 4 servings

1	pound pork tenderloin
1	tablespoon dried Italian seasoning, *McCormick®*
	Olive oil cooking spray, *Mazola® Pure*
1/4	cup Marsala wine
2	cups presliced mushrooms
1/2	tablespoon chopped garlic, *Christopher Ranch®*
1/2	cup organic chicken broth, *Swanson®*
1/4	cup light roasted garlic balsamic salad dressing, *Bernstein's®*
	Hot cooked spaghetti, *Barilla® Plus* (optional)
	Fresh oregano sprigs (optional)

1. Rinse tenderloin under cold water and pat dry with paper towels. Trim any fat and silver skin from pork. Slice into 8 pieces. Using the smooth side of a meat mallet or a small pot, pound pork pieces to a ½-inch thickness. Sprinkle both sides of pork pieces with Italian seasoning.

2. Coat a large skillet with cooking spray; heat over medium-high heat. Add pork; cook for 2 to 3 minutes per side or until cooked through. Transfer pork to a platter; cover with aluminum foil to keep warm.

3. Add Marsala wine to skillet and deglaze by scraping bits from bottom of skillet. Add mushrooms and garlic. Cook and stir on medium-high heat for 2 minutes. Add chicken broth and salad dressing; bring to a boil over high heat. Cook until mushrooms are tender. Reduce heat and return pork to skillet. Simmer for 3 to 4 minutes or until heated through.

4. Serve with hot cooked spaghetti and oregano (optional).

Per serving 187 cal., 6 g total fat (2 g sat. fat), 73 mg chol., 403 mg sodium, 4 g carbo., 1 g fiber, 26 g pro.
Daily Values 3% vit. C, 3% calcium, 13% iron

Pork Medallions with Brandied Apples

Start to Finish 25 minutes
Makes 4 servings

1	pound pork tenderloin
1	teaspoon garlic-pepper blend, *McCormick*®
½	teaspoon pumpkin pie spice, *McCormick*®
	Olive oil cooking spray, *Mazola*® *Pure*
¼	cup brandy, *Christian Brothers*®
2	cups presliced apples, *Chiquita*® *Fruit Bites*
½	cup organic chicken broth, *Swanson*®
2	tablespoons frozen apple juice concentrate, thawed, *Tree Top*®

SUPER FOODS
Apples

1. Rinse tenderloin under cold water and pat dry with paper towels. Trim any fat and silver skin from pork. Slice into 8 pieces. Using the smooth side of a mallet or a small pot, pound pork pieces to a ½-inch thickness. In a small bowl, combine garlic-pepper blend and pumpkin pie spice. Sprinkle both sides of pork pieces with spice mixture.

2. Coat a large skillet with cooking spray; heat over medium-high heat. Add pork; cook for 2 to 3 minutes per side or until pork is cooked through. Transfer pork to a platter; cover with aluminum foil to keep warm.

3. Add brandy to skillet and deglaze by scraping bits from bottom of skillet. Add apple slices, chicken broth, and apple juice concentrate. Cook over medium-high heat about 5 minutes or until apples are tender and liquid has thickened. Return pork to skillet; reduce heat. Simmer for 3 to 4 minutes or until heated through.

Per serving 214 cal., 3 g total fat (1 g sat. fat), 73 mg chol., 238 mg sodium, 11 g carbo., 1 g fiber, 25 g pro.
Daily Values 1% vit. A, 6% vit. C, 1% calcium, 9% iron

Sides & Accompaniments

Think of eating healthy as an adventure that encourages you to expand your food horizons by trying vegetables, grains, and fruits you wouldn't normally reach for. My nieces and nephews love twice-baked potatoes, so I notched up the nutrition with Twice-Baked Sweet Potatoes. I crave onion rings—but not all those calories!—so I switched to Balsamic Roasted Onions to get that creamy onion crunch minus the fried fat. And while baked beans still make it to the picnic, they're Best Black Beans, which keep the fiber and lose the sugar. Vibrant food stimulates the taste buds, so give plain foods a burst of color and flavor—acorn squash dressed up with raspberry stuffing, couscous salad brightened with sweet tomatoes, grilled vegetables on a canvas of saffron rice. Plant foods help you watch your weight, lower your blood pressure, and guard against strokes, heart attacks, and cancer. All good reasons to eat healthy.

The Recipes

Twice-Baked Sweet Potatoes

Prep 15 minutes **Bake** 1 hour + 15 minutes
Makes 4 servings

SUPER FOODS
Sweet potatoes
Pecans
Citrus

Olive oil cooking spray, *Mazola® Pure*
2 medium sweet potatoes
½ cup chopped pecans, *Planters®*
¼ cup packed brown sugar, *C&H®*
1 tablespoon frozen orange juice concentrate, thawed, *Dole®*
1 tablespoon butter, melted
1 teaspoon pumpkin pie spice, *McCormick®*

1. Preheat oven to 350 degrees F. Line a baking sheet with aluminum foil; coat with cooking spray. Set aside.

2. Wash sweet potatoes; pat dry with paper towels. Wrap each potato in aluminum foil. Bake in preheated oven for 1 hour or until a fork inserts easily into potato. Carefully remove foil; let stand until cool enough to handle. Cut each sweet potato in half horizontally. Without tearing skin, use a spoon to gently scoop out inside of sweet potato and place in medium bowl.

3. Set aside half of the pecans. Add the remaining pecans, brown sugar, orange juice concentrate, butter, and pumpkin pie spice to sweet potatoes in bowl. With a potato masher, mash potatoes until creamy. Divide mixture among hollowed-out potato halves. Sprinkle with reserved pecans. Place filled sweet potatoes on prepared baking sheet.

4. Bake sweet potatoes about 15 minutes or until heated through.

Per serving 239 cal., 13 g total fat (3 g sat. fat), 8 mg chol., 62 mg sodium, 31 g carbo., 3 g fiber, 5 g pro.
Daily Values 187% vit. A, 13% vit. C, 5% calcium, 6% iron

Honey-Chipotle Sweet Potatoes

Start to Finish 10 minutes
Makes 6 servings

2   cans (15 ounces each) sweet potatoes, drained, *Princella®*
2   tablespoons chipotle taco seasoning mix, *Ortega®*
2   tablespoons honey, *SueBee®*
2   teaspoons frozen orange juice concentrate, thawed, *Minute Maid®*
    Jalapeño chile pepper, chopped (see note, page 62) (optional)

SUPER FOODS
Sweet potatoes
Citrus

1. In a large microwave-safe bowl, combine sweet potatoes and taco seasoning mix. Cover and microwave on high setting (100% power) for 5 minutes. Stir in honey and orange juice. With a potato masher, mash sweet potatoes slightly. Garnish with chile pepper (optional).

Per serving 160 cal., 0 g total fat (0 g sat. fat), 0 mg chol., 219 mg sodium, 37 g carbo., 3 g fiber, 2 g pro.
Daily Values 226% vit. A, 67% vit. C, 3% calcium, 8% iron

Middle Eastern Potato Salad

Prep 10 minutes **Chill** 1 hour
Makes 6 servings

1   bag (16-ounce) precooked rosemary and garlic diced red-skin potatoes, *Reser's®*
½   cup fat-free plain yogurt, *Horizon Organic®*
2   scallions (green onions), chopped
2   tablespoons chopped pimientos, *Dromedary®*
2   tablespoons chopped fresh mint
2   tablespoons chopped fresh flat-leaf parsley or cilantro
1   jalapeño chile pepper, seeded and finely chopped (see note, page 62)
1   teaspoon minced garlic, *Christopher Ranch®*
1   teaspoon lemon juice, *ReaLemon®*
    Organic lemon wedges (optional)

SUPER FOODS
Yogurt
Onions
Chile peppers
Garlic
Citrus

1. In a medium bowl, combine potatoes, yogurt, scallions, pimientos, mint, parsley, chile pepper, garlic, and lemon juice. Chill in the refrigerator for 1 hour. Serve with lemon wedges (optional).

Per serving 137 cal., 2 g total fat (0 g sat. fat), 0 mg chol., 482 mg sodium, 22 g carbo., 2 g fiber, 4 g pro.
Daily Values 6% vit. A, 17% vit. C, 8% calcium, 8% iron

Roasted Potatoes of Provence

Prep 10 minutes **Bake** 30 minutes
Makes 4 servings

SUPER FOODS
Onion
Olive oil
Garlic

Olive oil cooking spray, *Mazola® Pure*
1 bag (16-ounce) precooked diced red-skin potatoes, *Reser's®*
1 scallion (green onion), thinly sliced
2 teaspoons extra-virgin olive oil, *Bertolli®*
1 teaspoon herbes de Provence, *McCormick®*
1 teaspoon crushed garlic, *Christopher Ranch®*
1 teaspoon Dijon mustard, *Grey Poupon®*

1. Preheat oven to 450 degrees F. Lightly coat a 13×9-inch baking dish with cooking spray.

2. In a large bowl, combine potatoes, scallion, olive oil, herbes de Provence, garlic, and mustard, tossing to coat potatoes. Transfer to prepared dish.

3. Roast potatoes in preheated oven for 30 to 40 minutes, turning potatoes halfway through cooking time.

SERVING IDEAS: Serve with Provençal Turkey Breast (see recipe, page 154).

Per serving 95 cal., 2 g total fat (0 g sat. fat), 0 mg chol., 150 mg sodium, 15 g carbo., 3 g fiber, 3 g pro.
Daily Values 1% vit. A, 8% vit. C, 1% calcium, 4% iron

Buttermilk-Garlic Smashed Potatoes

Start to Finish 20 minutes
Makes 6 servings

SUPER FOODS
Garlic

1 bag (16-ounce) fresh diced red-skin potatoes, *Reser's®*
1 cup buttermilk
4 cloves roasted whole garlic, finely chopped, *Christopher Ranch®*
4 teaspoons butter seasoning, *Molly McButter®*
½ cup low-fat sour cream, *Knudsen®*
Chopped chives (optional)

1. In a large microwave-safe bowl, combine potatoes, buttermilk, garlic, and butter seasoning. Cover; microwave on high setting (100% power) for 12 to 15 minutes, stirring halfway through cooking time.

2. Add sour cream. With a potato masher, mash potatoes until creamy but with lumps and peels visible. Garnish with chives (optional).

Per serving 119 cal., 2 g total fat (1 g sat. fat), 8 mg chol., 324 mg sodium, 20 g carbo., 2 g fiber, 5 g pro.
Daily Values 3% vit. A, 15% vit. C, 9% calcium, 2% iron

Red Beans-and-Rice Salad

Start to Finish 25 minutes
Makes 6 servings

1	can (14-ounce) organic chicken broth, *Swanson*®
1	box (6.2-ounce) quick-cooking long grain and wild rice, *Uncle Ben's*®
1	can (15-ounce) no-salt-added organic kidney beans, rinsed and drained, *Eden*®
1	cup chopped sweet onion
2	ribs celery, chopped
1	jar (4-ounce) chopped pimientos, drained, *Dromedary*®
¼	cup light balsamic vinegar salad dressing, *Newman's Own*®

SUPER FOODS
Beans
Onion

1. In small saucepan, combine chicken broth and rice with seasoning packet. Bring to a boil over high heat; reduce heat. Cover and simmer for 5 minutes. Remove from heat. Fluff with fork and spread on a baking sheet to cool.

2. In a large bowl, combine cooled rice, beans, onion, celery, pimientos, and salad dressing. Toss thoroughly. Serve at once or cover and chill in the refrigerator for up to 24 hours.

Per serving 194 cal., 2 g total fat (0 g sat. fat), 1 mg chol., 800 mg sodium, 37 g carbo., 7 g fiber, 8 g pro.
Daily Values 13% vit. A, 33% vit. C, 4% calcium, 13% iron

Grilled Vegetables with Saffron Rice

Start to Finish 30 minutes
Makes 6 servings

SUPER FOODS
Peppers
Almonds

$1\frac{2}{3}$ cups low-sodium chicken broth, *Swanson*®
1   packet (5-ounce) saffron-flavored rice, *Mahatma*®
    Canola oil cooking spray, *Mazola® Pure*
1   pound fresh asparagus, woody ends removed
2   medium red bell peppers, cut into 1-inch pieces
1   zucchini, cut into $\frac{1}{4}$-inch slices
1   teaspoon capers, drained
$\frac{1}{4}$ cup slivered almonds, toasted, *Planters*®

1. In a large saucepan, bring chicken broth to a boil over high heat. Add rice; reduce heat to low. Cover; simmer for 20 minutes or until rice is fluffy.

2. Set up grill for direct cooking over medium-high heat. Coat a grill pan with cooking spray. Preheat pan. Working in batches, place asparagus, peppers, and zucchini on pan and grill just until tender. Use tongs to remove from heat. Cut zucchini and asparagus into bite-size pieces.

3. In a large bowl, toss together rice, grilled vegetables, and capers. Top with toasted almonds.

Per serving 141 cal., 3 g total fat (0 g sat. fat), 0 mg chol., 486 mg sodium, 25 g carbo., 5 g fiber, 6 g pro.
Daily Values 32% vit. A, 146% vit. C, 3% calcium, 14% iron

Smoky Spanish Rice

Prep 5 minutes **Cook** 20 minutes
Stand 5 minutes **Makes** 6 servings

3 ⅓   cups water
1 ½   cups converted long grain rice, *Uncle Ben's*®
1   can (14.5-ounce) diced tomatoes, *Hunt's*®
1   can (4-ounce) diced green chiles, drained, *Ortega*®
2   tablespoons chipotle taco seasoning mix, *Ortega*®

SUPER FOODS
Tomatoes
Chile peppers

1. In a large saucepan, combine water, rice, tomatoes, green chiles, and taco seasoning mix. Bring to a boil over high heat; reduce heat to low. Cover and simmer for 20 minutes. Remove from heat. Let stand, covered, for 5 minutes. Fluff with a fork and serve.

Per serving 193 cal., 0 g total fat (0 g sat. fat), 0 mg chol., 426 mg sodium, 42 g carbo., 0 g fiber, 5 g pro.
Daily Values 2% vit. A, 27% vit. C, 9% calcium, 12% iron

Sesame Brown Rice

Start to Finish 20 minutes
Makes 4 servings

1 ¾   cups vegetable broth, *Health Valley*®
1   cup quick-cooking brown rice, *Uncle Ben's*®
2   tablespoons Chinese chicken salad dressing mix, *Kikkoman*®
¼   to ½ teaspoon red pepper flakes, *McCormick*®
1   scallion (green onion), bias sliced
2   tablespoons sesame seeds
2   teaspoons toasted sesame oil
       Scallions (green onion), slivered (optional)

SUPER FOODS
Whole grains
Chile peppers
Onions

1. In a medium saucepan, combine vegetable broth, rice, salad dressing mix, and pepper flakes. Bring to a boil over high heat; reduce heat to low. Cover and simmer for 10 minutes or until all of the liquid is absorbed. Remove from heat. Fluff rice with a fork. Stir in bias-sliced scallion, sesame seeds, and sesame oil. Garnish with slivered scallions (optional).

Per serving 165 cal., 5 g total fat (1 g sat. fat), 0 mg chol., 432 mg sodium, 27 g carbo., 2 g fiber, 3 g pro.
Daily Values 1% vit. A, 1% vit. C, 7% calcium, 5% iron

Tomato-Couscous Salad

Start to Finish 25 minutes
Makes 6 servings

SUPER FOODS
Onions
Tomatoes

Tomatoes are loaded with disease-fighting nutrients. Toss cherry tomatoes with health-conscious couscous for a summery Mediterranean-style side.

	Olive oil cooking spray, *Mazola® Pure*
1 ¼	cups vegetable broth, *Health Valley®*
1	cup tomato-flavored couscous, *Rice Selects®*
½	pound thin asparagus spears, cut into 1-inch pieces
2	scallions (green onions), sliced
3	tablespoons light Italian salad dressing, *Newman's Own®*
1	cup cherry tomatoes, halved
¼	cup finely chopped fresh basil
	Bibb lettuce leaves (optional)

1. Preheat oven to 400 degrees F. Lightly coat baking sheet with cooking spray; set aside.

2. In a small pot, bring vegetable broth to a boil. Stir in couscous. Remove from heat and cover. Let stand for 5 minutes. Fluff with fork; set aside.

3. Place asparagus and scallions on prepared baking sheet. Toss with 1 tablespoon of the salad dressing. Roast in preheated oven for 10 to 12 minutes.

4. In a large bowl, combine cooked couscous, roasted vegetables, cherry tomatoes, basil, and remaining salad dressing. Toss to combine. Divide among lettuce leaves (optional). Serve warm or at room temperature.

Per serving 131 cal., 1 g total fat (0 g sat. fat), 0 mg chol., 141 mg sodium, 25 g carbo., 1 g fiber, 4 g pro.
Daily Values 14% vit. A, 12% vit. C, 2% calcium, 6% iron

Best Black Beans

Start to Finish 20 minutes
Makes 4 servings

1	can (15-ounce) no-salt-added organic black beans, rinsed and drained, *Eden*®
1	can (10-ounce) diced tomatoes with chiles in sauce, *Ro-Tel*®
½	cup frozen chopped onions, *Ore-Ida*®
¼	cup finely chopped fresh cilantro
1	tablespoon lime juice, *ReaLime*®
1	teaspoon crushed garlic, *Christopher Ranch*®

SUPER FOODS
Beans
Tomatoes
Onions
Citrus
Garlic

1. In a medium saucepan, combine beans, tomatoes, onions, cilantro, lime juice, and garlic. Bring to a boil over medium-high heat; reduce heat to low. Simmer for 10 minutes.

Per serving 130 cal., 1 g total fat (0 g sat. fat), 10 mg chol., 336 mg sodium, 20 g carbo., 6 g fiber, 10 g pro.
Daily Values 14% vit. A, 18% vit. C, 7% calcium, 13% iron

Balsamic Roasted Onions

Prep 10 minutes **Marinate** 1 hour **Stand** 30 minutes
Bake 25 minutes **Makes** 6 servings

SUPER FOODS
Onions
Garlic

3	**sweet onions**
1	**cup light balsamic salad dressing, Newman's Own®**
2	**tablespoons chopped fresh tarragon**
½	**teaspoon crushed garlic, Christopher Ranch®**
	Olive oil cooking spray, *Mazola® Pure*
	Ground black pepper, *McCormick®*

1. Cut ends off onions making sure core is left intact. Quarter onions through core and peel away skin. Place onions in a large zip-top plastic bag.

2. For marinade, in a bowl, combine salad dressing, tarragon, and garlic. Pour in zip-top bag with onions. Squeeze air from bag and seal. Gently massage bag to combine ingredients. Marinate in the refrigerator for 1 to 4 hours, turning occasionally.

3. Remove onions from the refrigerator 30 minutes before roasting. Preheat oven to 400 degrees F. Lightly coat a baking pan with cooking spray; set aside.

4. Remove onions from zip-top bag; place, cut sides up, in prepared baking pan. Pour marinade over onions. Season with pepper.

5. Roast onions in preheated oven for 25 minutes or until fork tender. (If onions brown too quickly, cover loosely with aluminum foil.)

Per serving 97 cal., 5 g total fat (1 g sat. fat), 0 mg chol., 629 mg sodium, 12 g carbo., 1 g fiber, 1 g pro.
Daily Values 9% vit. C, 2% calcium, 1% iron

Acorn Squash with Raspberry Stuffing

Prep 15 minutes **Bake** 45 minutes + 15 minutes
Makes 4 servings

SUPER FOODS
Olive oil
Whole grains
Raspberries
Walnuts
Onion
Citrus

1	large acorn squash
2	teaspoons extra-virgin olive oil, *Bertolli®*
¼	teaspoon pumpkin pie spice, *McCormick®*
1	cup cooked brown rice, *Uncle Ben's® Ready Rice*
½	cup frozen raspberries, *Dole®*
¼	cup chopped walnuts, *Planters®*
¼	cup light raspberry and walnut vinaigrette, *Newman's Own®*
1	scallion (green onion), finely chopped
1	tablespoon frozen orange juice concentrate, thawed, *Minute Maid®*

1. Preheat oven to 400 degrees F. Cut squash in half and scoop out seeds. Brush cut surface of squash with olive oil; sprinkle with pumpkin pie spice. Set aside.

2. In a large bowl, combine rice, raspberries, walnuts, salad dressing, scallion, and orange juice concentrate. Spoon mixture into centers of squash. Place in a baking dish and cover with aluminum foil.

3. Bake squash in preheated oven for 45 minutes. Remove foil; bake 15 to 20 minutes more or until squash is fork tender. To serve, cut each squash half in half.

Per serving 228 cal., 11 g total fat (1 g sat. fat), 0 mg chol., 66 mg sodium, 32 g carbo., 4 g fiber, 4 g pro.
Daily Values 10% vit. A, 35% vit. C, 6% calcium, 9% iron

Gold and Green Salad

Start to Finish 15 minutes
Makes 4 servings

This two-tone salad doubles up on the disease-fighting antioxidants found in green and yellow fruits and vegetables. Just drizzle avocados, mangoes, and salad greens with lemon dressing and garnish with scallions.

SUPER FOODS
Citrus
Mango
Avocado
Onion

FOR DRESSING:

1/4	cup light mayonnaise, *Hellmann's® or Best Foods®*
1/4	cup fat-free sour cream, *Knudsen®*
1	tablespoon lemon juice, *ReaLemon®*
1/2	teaspoon reduced-sodium soy sauce, *Kikkoman®*

FOR SALAD:

4	cups spring salad mix, *Fresh Express®*
12	refrigerated mango slices, drained, *Ready Pac®*
1	avocado, sliced into 12 slices
12	slices cucumber (optional)
1/4	cup bias-sliced scallions (green onions)

1. For Dressing, in a small bowl, stir together mayonnaise, sour cream, lemon juice, and soy sauce; set aside.

2. For Salad, divide salad mix among 4 chilled salad plates. Divide mango, avocado, and cucumber slices (optional) among plates. Spoon dressing over salads; sprinkle with scallions.

Per serving 208 cal., 11 g total fat (1 g sat. fat), 6 mg chol., 164 mg sodium, 29 g carbo., 4 g fiber, 2 g pro.
Daily Values 29% vit. A, 76% vit. C, 5% calcium, 4% iron

Sweet and Spicy Slaw

Prep 10 minutes **Chill** 1 hour
Makes 6 servings

SUPER FOODS
Broccoli
Onion
Yogurt
Chile peppers

1 package (12-ounce) broccoli slaw (or 4 cups coleslaw mix), *The Produce Stand*®
¼ cup chopped red onion
⅔ cup fat-free plain yogurt, *Horizon Organic*®
¼ cup honey, *SueBee*®
2 tablespoons cider vinegar, *Heinz*®
2 tablespoons chopped jalapeño chile peppers, drained, (see note, page 62) *Ortega*®
Salt and ground black pepper

1. In a large bowl, combine broccoli slaw and red onion; set aside.

2. In a small bowl, stir together yogurt, honey, vinegar, and chile peppers. Pour over broccoli slaw mixture, tossing to combine. Season with salt and black pepper. Chill in the refrigerator for 1 hour.

Per serving 79 cal., 0 g total fat (0 g sat. fat), 1 mg chol., 134 mg sodium, 18 g carbo., 2 g fiber, 3 g pro.
Daily Values 34% vit. A, 82% vit. C, 8% calcium, 4% iron

Desserts

Dessert is what you make it. I grew up picking cherries from the orchard across the street and strawberries, blueberries, raspberries, and blackberries from fields and patches near my home. Occasionally I'd use them in shortcake or cobbler—even jams, but most of the time, my sisters and brothers and I ate them by the handful, enjoying every bite of their simple goodness. We considered them a treat! This chapter is filled with such treats, which are far from a nutritional zero. Pears with Almonds and Chantilly Cream contributes a serving of fruit and low-fat dairy and protein too. Deep, dark, delicious chocolate produces feel-good serotonin—all the more reason to give dinner a happy ending with a warm Super Moist Chocolate Cake with Chocolate-Cinnamon Mousse or cool Chocolate-Hazelnut Sorbet. Every spoonful is a sweet indulgence that has been slimmed down to reduce the fat and sugar.

The Recipes

Super Moist Chocolate Cake with Chocolate-Cinnamon Mousse

Prep 25 minutes **Bake** 45 minutes
Makes 12 servings

SUPER FOODS
Apples
Eggs
Soy
Cinnamon

FOR CHOCOLATE CAKE:

	Canola oil cooking spray, *Mazola® Pure*
3	medium zucchini, finely grated (about 3 cups)
1	package (18.25-ounce) chocolate fudge cake mix, *Betty Crocker®*
1½	cups organic applesauce, *Santa Cruz®*
5	large egg whites
¾	cup fat-free plain yogurt, *Horizon Organic®*

FOR CHOCOLATE-CINNAMON MOUSSE:

1	cup fat-free milk
1	block (12.25-ounce) soft silken tofu, *Mori-Nu®*
1	box (3.9-ounce) instant chocolate fudge pudding mix, *Jell-O®*
1	tablespoon ground cinnamon, *McCormick®*
	Whole fresh strawberries (optional)
	Powdered sugar, *C&H®* (optional)

1. For Chocolate Cake, preheat oven to 350 degrees F. Lightly coat only the bottom of a 13×9-inch cake pan with cooking spray.

2. In a large mixing bowl, combine zucchini, cake mix, applesauce, egg whites, and yogurt. Beat on low speed of an electric mixer for 2 minutes, scraping side of bowl often. Pour into prepared pan.

3. Bake in preheated oven for 45 to 50 minutes or until toothpick inserted into center of cake comes out clean. Cool cake in pan on a wire rack.

4. For Chocolate-Cinnamon Mousse, place milk in a blender; add tofu. Cover and blend on high until smooth.

5. In a small mixing bowl, combine milk mixture, pudding mix, and cinnamon. Beat on low speed of an electric mixer for 2 minutes. Cover and refrigerate until ready to use.

6. To serve, cut Chocolate Cake into individual servings. Spoon some of the Chocolate-Cinnamon Mousse over each serving. Garnish with strawberries (optional). Dust with powdered sugar (optional).

Per serving 276 cal., 4 g total fat (1 g sat. fat), 1 mg chol., 508 mg sodium, 55 g carbo., 2 g fiber, 7 g pro.
Daily Values 3% vit. A, 15% vit. C, 12% calcium, 12% iron

Kahlúa-Coffee Angel Food Cake

Prep 25 minutes **Bake** 37 minutes
Stand 1 hour **Makes** 12 servings

1	cup plus 1 tablespoon cold water
3	tablespoons coffee liqueur, *Kahlúa*®
1	tablespoon instant coffee crystals, *Folgers*®
1	box (16-ounce) angel food cake mix, *Betty Crocker*®
2	tablespoons unsweetened cocoa powder, *Hershey's*®
1	box (1-pound) powdered sugar, sifted, *C&H*®
¼	cup coffee liqueur, *Kahlúa*®
¼	cup fat-free milk
3	tablespoons unsweetened cocoa powder, *Hershey's*®
1	tablespoon instant coffee crystals, *Folgers*®
	Fresh raspberries (optional)
	Sifted powdered sugar, *C&H*® (optional)

SUPER FOODS
Cocoa

1. Move oven rack to lowest position. Preheat oven to 350 degrees F.

2. In large mixing bowl, combine cold water, the 3 tablespoons coffee liqueur, and 1 tablespoon coffee crystals, stirring until coffee dissolves. Add cake mix and the 2 tablespoons cocoa powder. Beat mixture on low speed of an electric mixer for 30 seconds. Scrape down side of bowl; beat on medium speed for 1 minute. Pour into ungreased 10×4-inch tube pan.

3. Bake in preheated oven for 37 to 47 minutes or until top is dark golden brown, cracked, and not sticky to the touch. Immediately invert pan onto a wine bottle; cool completely.

4. For icing, in a medium bowl, stir together the box of powdered sugar, the ¼ cup coffee liqueur, milk, cocoa powder, and 1 tablespoon coffee crystals. Run a table knife around edges of cake and remove cake from pan. Pour icing evenly over cake, letting it run down the sides. Let cake stand for at least 1 hour to allow icing to set.

5. To serve, cut cake into individual servings. Top with raspberries (optional) and sprinkle with additional powdered sugar (optional).

Per serving 331 cal., 0 g total fat (0 g sat. fat), 0 mg chol., 322 mg sodium, 74 g carbo., 0 g fiber, 4 g pro.
Daily Values 9% calcium, 2% iron

Nuts and Berries
Angel Food Cake

Prep 25 minutes **Bake** 28 minutes
Stand 30 minutes **Makes** 8 servings

SUPER FOODS
Berries
Almonds

1   package (16-ounce) angel food cake mix, *Betty Crocker*®
1¼   cups water
1   teaspoon almond extract, *McCormick*®
3   cups fat-free frozen whipped topping, thawed, *Cool Whip*®
1½   cups fresh or frozen whole strawberries, halved, *Cascadian Farm*®
1½   cups fresh or frozen organic blueberries, *Cascadian Farm*®
¼   cup hazelnut liqueur, *Frangelico*®
½   cup sliced almonds, toasted, *Planters*®

1. Move oven rack to middle position. Preheat oven to 350 degrees F.

2. In a large mixing bowl, combine cake mix and water. Beat on low speed of an electric mixer for 30 seconds. Scrape down side of bowl; beat on medium speed for 1 minute. Pour batter into 2 ungreased 9×5×3-inch loaf pans.

3. Bake in preheated oven for 28 to 32 minutes. Remove and place loaf pans upside down on a wire rack. Cool completely.

4. Carefully stir almond extract into thawed whipped topping. Refrigerate until ready to use.

5. In a medium bowl, stir together strawberries, blueberries, and hazelnut liqueur. Let stand at room temperature for 30 minutes to 1 hour.

6. To serve, cut each cake into 8 slices. Place one cake slice on each of 8 dessert plates. Top each with 2 tablespoons fruit mixture and 1 tablespoon of whipped topping mixture. Add a second cake slice to each plate. Top each with 2 additional tablespoons of fruit mixture and 1 tablespoon whipped topping mixture. Sprinkle each serving with almonds.*

*NOTE: For a lighter dessert, serve only one slice of cake topped by 2 tablespoons of the fruit mixture, 1 tablespoon whipped topping, and some of the almonds.

Per serving 376 cal., 5 g total fat (0 g sat. fat), 0 mg chol., 501 mg sodium, 73 g carbo., 2 g fiber, 7 g pro.
Daily Values 8% vit. C, 12% calcium, 3% iron

Triple Raspberry Brownies

Prep 25 minutes **Bake** 30 minutes
Makes 16 servings

A classic favorite gets a boost from fiber-rich raspberries. Prunes, organic applesauce, and raspberry spreadable fruit combine with a boxed brownie mix to render a more healthful treat; a raspberry coulis and garnish make it extra tasty.

SUPER FOODS
Apples
Eggs
Raspberries

FOR BROWNIES:
- Butter-flavor cooking spray, *Mazola® Pure*
- ½ cup dried plums (prunes), *Sunsweet®*
- ⅓ cup unsweetened organic applesauce, *Santa Cruz®*
- 1 box (19.5-ounce) brownie mix, *Betty Crocker®*
- 2 egg whites
- ¼ cup framboise or other raspberry liqueur
- ⅓ cup raspberry spreadable fruit, *Dickinson's®*

FOR RASPBERRY COULIS:
- 2 cups frozen raspberries, thawed, *Dole®*
- 2 tablespoons framboise or other raspberry liqueur
- 1 tablespoon honey
- Fresh raspberries (optional)
- Fresh mint sprig (optional)

1. For Brownies, preheat oven to 350 degrees F. Lightly coat a 9×9-inch baking pan with cooking spray; set aside.

2. Place dried plums and applesauce in a blender. Cover and blend on high until smooth.

3. In a medium bowl, combine fruit mixture, brownie mix, egg whites, and the ¼ cup framboise. Using a wooden spoon, stir 50 strokes. Transfer to prepared baking pan; set aside.

4. In a small saucepan, heat spreadable fruit over medium-high heat until melted. Drizzle over mixture in baking pan. Swirl with a table knife.

5. Bake in preheated oven for 30 to 35 minutes. Cool completely in pan on wire rack. Cut into squares.

6. For Raspberry Coulis, place frozen raspberries, the 2 tablespoons framboise, and honey in a blender. Cover and blend on high speed until pureed. To remove seeds, push mixture through a fine-mesh strainer; set aside. Discard seeds.

7. For each serving, spoon 1 to 2 tablespoons Raspberry Coulis on a dessert plate. Top with a Brownie. Serve with fresh raspberries and mint (optional).

Per serving 207 cal., 5 g total fat (1 g sat. fat), 0 mg chol., 112 mg sodium, 38 g carbo., 1 g fiber, 2 g pro.
Daily Values 1% vit. A, 3% vit. C, 1% calcium, 5% iron

Cherry Flan

Prep 20 minutes **Chill** 1 hour
Makes 8 servings

SUPER FOODS
Cherries

1   **box (5.5-ounce) flan mix with caramel sauce,** *Royal*®
½   **teaspoon cherry extract,** *McCormick*®
1   **cup frozen cherries, thawed and chopped,** *Dole*®
4   **cups low-fat milk**
1   **teaspoon almond extract,** *McCormick*®
     Maraschino cherries with stems (optional)
     Fresh mint sprigs (optional)

1. Remove pouch of caramel sauce from flan mix. In a small bowl, stir together caramel sauce and cherry extract. Divide mixture among eight 6-ounce ramekins. Divide chopped cherries among ramekins; set aside.

2. In medium saucepan, stir together flan mix, milk, and almond extract. Bring to a full boil over medium-high heat, stirring constantly. Using a ladle, carefully divide flan mixture among ramekins. (Mixture will thicken as it cools.) Chill in the refrigerator for at least 1 hour.

3. To serve, run the tip of a table knife around the edge of each ramekin to loosen flan. Place a dessert plate upside down over ramekin. Invert plate and ramekin. Remove ramekin. Garnish with maraschino cherries with stems and mint (optional).

Per serving 150 cal., 2 g total fat (1 g sat. fat), 13 mg chol., 83 mg sodium, 28 g carbo., 0 g fiber, 4 g pro.
Daily Values 5% vit. A, 2% vit. C, 15% calcium, 1% iron

Lime Soufflé

Prep 20 minutes **Bake** 20 minutes
Makes 4 servings

Butter-flavor cooking spray, *Mazola® Pure*
Granulated sugar
$\frac{1}{3}$ cup lime curd, *Dickinson's®*
1 container (99 grams) fat-free vanilla pudding, *Kraft® Handi-Snacks*
4 egg whites
2 thin organic lime slices, halved (optional)
Granulated sugar (optional)
Powdered sugar, *C&H®*

SUPER FOODS
Citrus
Eggs

1. Preheat oven to 400 degrees F. Coat four 6-ounce ramekins with cooking spray. Lightly coat the inside of each ramekin with granulated sugar; set aside.

2. In a small bowl, stir together lime curd and vanilla pudding; set aside.

3. In large mixing bowl, beat egg whites on high spread of an electric mixer until stiff peaks form (tips stand straight). Stir one-fourth of the egg whites into the lime curd mixture. Spoon lime curd mixture into bowl with egg whites and gently fold just until combined. Divide mixture among ramekins. Place ramekins on a baking sheet.

4. Bake in preheated oven for 20 minutes or until risen and golden brown. Meanwhile, coat both sides of lime slices with granulated sugar (optional).

5. To serve, dust soufflé with powdered sugar and serve immediately. Garnish with sugared lime slices (optional).

Per serving 135 cal., 1 g total fat (1 g sat. fat), 20 mg chol., 121 mg sodium, 24 g carbo., 0 g fiber, 4 g pro.
Daily Values 1% vit. A, 2% calcium, 1% iron

Spiced Peach and Cranberry Phyllo Cups

Start to Finish 30 minutes
Makes 6 servings

SUPER FOODS
Soy
Cinnamon
Cranberries

Butter-flavor cooking spray, *Mazola® Pure*
1   **package (8-ounce) phyllo dough,** *Athens®*
1½ **cups light soymilk,** *Soy Dream®*
1   **package (1-ounce) sugar-free, fat-free white chocolate instant pudding and pie filling mix,** *Jell-O®*
¼   **teaspoon ground cinnamon,** *McCormick®*
¼   **teaspoon almond extract,** *McCormick®*
2   **cans (8.25 ounces each) raspberry-flavored chunky peaches, drained,** *Del Monte®*
1   **cup fat-free frozen whipped topping, thawed,** *Cool Whip®*
2   **tablespoons dried cranberries, chopped,** *Sun-Maid®*

1. Preheat oven to 350 degrees F. Coat six 2½-inch muffin cups with cooking spray; set aside.

2. Coat 5 sheets of phyllo dough with cooking spray. Stack sheets; with a knife, cut sheets into 5-inch squares. Fit cut squares into muffin cups. (Coat and stack another 5 sheets, if necessary.) Tightly wrap and refreeze any unused phyllo dough.

3. Bake phyllo cups in preheated oven for 8 to 10 minutes or until lightly browned. Cool completely in muffin cups on a wire rack.

4. In a medium bowl, whisk together soymilk and pudding mix about 2 minutes or until pudding thickens. Stir in cinnamon and almond extract. Cover and refrigerate for 5 to 10 minutes or until pudding is set. Stir in peaches.

5. Spoon mixture into phyllo cups. Top each cup with some of the whipped topping. Sprinkle each with some of the cranberries.

Per serving 221 cal., 3 g total fat (1 g sat. fat), 0 mg chol., 367 mg sodium, 44 g carbo., 1 g fiber, 4 g pro.
Daily Values 5% vit. A, 4% vit. C, 8% calcium, 10% iron

Lemon Kisses

Prep 25 minutes **Stand** 30 minutes + 30 minutes
Bake 32 minutes **Makes** 3 dozen

Instead of fast-food desserts, pick up some fast fruit and dole out the kisses to serve alongside. As light and fluffy as meringues, these luscious lemon drops are made with egg whites to keep cholesterol in check.

SUPER FOODS
Eggs
Citrus

4	**large egg whites**
1	**teaspoon grated lemon zest**
$\frac{1}{8}$	**teaspoon salt**
$\frac{1}{8}$	**teaspoon lemon juice, *ReaLemon*®**
1	**cup sugar**
1	**teaspoon vanilla extract, *McCormick*®**
$\frac{1}{2}$	**teaspoon lemon extract, *McCormick*®**
3	**drops yellow food coloring, *McCormick*®**

1. Let egg whites stand at room temperature for 30 minutes. Preheat oven to 250 degrees F. Line 2 baking sheets with parchment paper.

2. In a medium mixing bowl, combine egg whites, lemon zest, salt, and lemon juice. Beat on low speed of an electric mixer about 30 seconds or until foamy. Beat on high speed about 1 minute or until frothy. Gradually add sugar, beating until combined. Scrape down side of bowl as needed. Add vanilla extract, lemon extract, and food coloring. Beat on medium speed until stiff peaks form (tips stand straight). Mixture will be glossy.

3. Place the mixture in a pastry bag fitted with ½-inch star tip. Pipe kisses onto prepared baking sheets, spacing them 1½ inches apart. Place both baking sheets in preheated oven.

4. Bake for 16 to 18 minutes. Rotate sheets front to back and top to bottom. Bake 16 to 18 minutes more. Turn off oven and let kisses stand in oven for 30 minutes.

5. Remove baking sheets from oven. Transfer parchment paper with kisses from baking sheet to a flat surface. Cool completely. Gently peel the kisses from parchment paper.

Per kiss 24 cal., 0 g total fat (0 g sat. fat), 0 mg chol., 14 mg sodium, 5 g carbo., 0 g fiber, 0 g pro.

Pears with Almonds and Chantilly Cream

Start to Finish 10 minutes
Makes 4 servings

SUPER FOODS
Almonds

1   package (14-ounce) fat-free vanilla pudding cups (4 cups), *Kraft® Handi-Snacks*
1   container (8-ounce) fat-free frozen whipped topping, thawed, *Cool Whip®*
1   teaspoon almond extract, *McCormick®*
2   cans (15.25 ounces each) light pear halves, *Del Monte®*
¼   cup sliced almonds, toasted, *Planters®*

1. For chantilly cream, in a medium bowl, combine pudding, whipped topping, and almond extract.

2. To serve, arrange 3 pears halves in each of 4 serving dishes. Top each with chantilly cream and sprinkle with almonds.

Per serving 346 cal., 5 g total fat (0 g sat. fat), 1 mg chol., 271 mg sodium, 70 g carbo., 3 g fiber, 4 g pro.
Daily Values 3% vit. A, 7% vit. C, 8% calcium, 4% iron

Apricot Compote

Start to Finish 10 minutes
Makes 6 servings

SUPER FOODS
Citrus

1   can (15-ounce) light apricot halves, *Del Monte®*
1   cup dried apricots, cut into thin strips, *Sun-Maid®*
¼   cup golden raisins
1   tablespoon lemon juice, *ReaLemon®*
2   teaspoons finely chopped fresh mint
3   cups fat-free vanilla ice cream

1. In a medium saucepan, combine apricots, raisins, lemon juice, and mint. Slowly cook over medium-high heat until liquid is almost gone and dried fruit is rehydrated. Serve warm with ice cream.

Per serving 209 cal., 0 g total fat (0 g sat. fat), 0 mg chol., 74 mg sodium, 52 g carbo., 3 g fiber, 5 g pro.
Daily Values 33% vit. A, 7% vit. C, 8% calcium, 6% iron

Berries with Champagne Sabayon

Prep 10 minutes **Stand** 30 minutes
Makes 6 servings

1 ¼	cups extra-dry champagne, *Korbel*®
¼	cup honey
1	package (16-ounce) frozen mixed berries, thawed, *Dole*®
3	teaspoons grated orange zest
¼	cup fresh orange juice
1	package (12.5-ounce) silken extra-firm tofu, *Mori-Nu*®
	Orange zest curls (optional)

SUPER FOODS
Berries
Citrus
Soy

1. In a glass measuring cup, combine ½ cup of the champagne and 2 tablespoons of the honey, stirring until honey dissolves. In a small bowl, pour champagne mixture over berries. Stir 2 teaspoons of the grated orange zest and the orange juice into berry mixture. Let stand at room temperature for 30 minutes to 1 hour.

2. For champagne sabayon, place remaining ¾ cup champagne into a blender. Add tofu, the remaining 2 tablespoons honey, and the remaining 1 teaspoon grated orange zest. Cover and blend on high until smooth. Refrigerate until ready to serve.

3. To serve, divide berry mixture among 6 champagne flutes. Top with champagne sabayon. Garnish with orange zest curls (optional).

Per serving 159 cal., 1 g total fat (0 g sat. fat), 0 mg chol., 38 mg sodium, 26 g carbo., 3 g fiber, 5 g pro.
Daily Values 19% vit. C, 3% calcium, 8% iron

Chocolate-Hazelnut Sorbet

Prep 30 minutes **Chill** 1 hour
Freeze per manufacturer's directions
Makes 6 servings

2	cups hot water
6	decaffeinated chocolate-hazelnut tea bags
½	cup chocolate-flavored syrup, *Hershey's*®
2	tablespoons hazelnut liqueur, *Frangelico*®
2	teaspoons instant espresso powder, *Medaglia D'Oro*®
	Fresh raspberries (optional)
	Cookie wafers (optional)

1. In a small saucepan, bring water to a boil over high heat. Remove from heat and add tea bags; let stand for 5 minutes. Remove and discard tea bags.

2. In a large bowl, combine tea mixture, chocolate-flavored syrup, hazelnut liqueur, and espresso powder. Cool to room temperature. Chill in the refrigerator about 1 hour or until thoroughly chilled.

3. Freeze tea mixture in a 1½-quart ice cream freezer according to the manufacturer's directions.

4. Serve with raspberries and cookie wafers (optional).

Per serving 89 cal., 0 g total fat (0 g sat. fat), 0 mg chol., 20 mg sodium, 18 g carbo., 1 g fiber, 1 g pro.
Daily Values 1% calcium, 3% iron

Index

Index

Free
Lifestyle web magazine subscription

Just visit
www.semi-homemade.com
today to subscribe!

Sign yourself and your friends and family up to the semi-homemaker's club today!

Each online issue is filled with fast, easy how-to projects, simple lifestyle solutions, and an abundance of helpful hints and terrific tips. It's the complete go-to magazine for busy people on-the-move.

tables & settings   fashion & beauty   ideas   home & garden   fabulous florals

super suppers   perfect parties   great gatherings   decadent desserts

gifts & giving   details   wines & music   fun favors   semi-homemaker's club

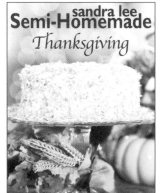

Semi-Homemade.com
making life easier, better, and more enjoyable

Semihomemade.com has hundreds of ways to simplify your life—the easy Semi-Homemade way! You'll find fast ways to de-clutter, try your hand at clever crafts, create terrific tablescapes or decorate indoors and out to make your home and garden superb with style.

We're especially proud of our Semi-Homemakers club: a part of semi-homemade.com which hosts other semihomemakers just like you. The club community shares ideas to make life easier, better, and more manageable with smart tips and hints allowing you time to do what you want! Sign-up and join today—it's free—and sign up your friends and family, too! It's easy the Semi-Homemade way! Visit the site today and start enjoying your busy life!

Sign yourself and your friends and family up to the semi-homemaker's club today!

tablescapes   home   garden   organizing   crafts

everyday & special days   cooking   entertaining   cocktail time

Halloween   Thanksgiving   Christmas   Valentine's   Easter   New Year's

About Sandra Lee

Sandra Lee is a *New York Times* best-selling author and a nationally acclaimed lifestyle expert. Her signature Semi-Homemade approach to cooking, home decorating, gardening, crafting, entertaining, beauty, and fashion offers savvy shortcuts and down-to-earth secrets for creating a beautiful, affordable, and most importantly doable lifestyle.

Sandra Lee's cookbook series offers amazing meals in minutes, fabulous food fixin's, and sensational—yet simple—style ideas. *Semi-Homemade Cooking with Sandra Lee* is one of Food Network's hottest cooking shows, providing many helpful hints, timesaving techniques, tips, and tricks.

Find even more sensible, savvy solutions online at **semihomemade.com**.

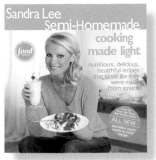

Sandra Lee Semi-Homemade® Cookbook Series
Collect all these amazingly helpful, timesaving, and beautiful books!
Look for the series wherever quality books are sold.